A Companion to
The Waterloo Declaration

A Companion to The Waterloo Declaration

Commentary and Essays on Lutheran–Anglican Relations in Canada

Edited by Richard G. Leggett

on behalf of The Anglican–Lutheran Joint Working Group
March 1999

Anglican Book Centre
Toronto, Canada

1999
Anglican Book Centre
600 Jarvis Streeet
Toronto, Ontario
M4Y 2J6

© 1999 The Joint Working Group of the Anglican Church of Canada and the Evangelical Lutheran Church in Canada

Canadian Cataloguing in Publication data is available from the National Library.

Contents

Editor's Preface

Among its various connotations, "companion" counts "someone to break bread with." Since 1989 Lutherans and Anglicans in Canada have been doing just that: breaking the Bread of Life together. In the breaking of bread we have discovered that we are not as different as we may have thought we were. Even our differences have served to open windows into the mystery of the triune God who calls us into koinonia with the One in whom and from whom we have our being.

The commentary and essays that follow speak in various voices: the Joint Working Group, seminary faculty, national staff members, and persons engaged directly in the day to day mission and ministry of our two churches. The Joint Working Group hopes that the variety of voices will help the members of our two churches better understand our hope that the first year of the new millennium will witness the declaration of full communion between Anglicans and Lutherans in Canada.

The "Commentary on The Waterloo Declaration" represents the views of the Joint Working Group. In it we set forth our understanding of the principles that have guided us in the formulation of the Waterloo Declaration.

The essays that follow the commentary focus on Anglican and Lutheran history as well as issues in the theology of ministry that have, in the eyes of some, kept us apart. Some of these essays are formal, while others are more personal. Regardless of style, all the authors have a common goal: the bringing together of two great reform movements of the Catholic church into a greater degree of visible unity and into a new dimension of our common mission and ministry.

Richard G. Leggett
on behalf of The Anglican–Lutheran Joint Working Group
March 1999

Contributors

ALYSON BARNETT-COWAN (Anglican) is Director of Faith, Worship and Ministry of the Anglican Church of Canada in Toronto, Ontario.

JOHN FLYNN (Anglican) is Professor of Systematic Theology at the College of Emmanuel and Saint Chad in Saskatoon, Saskatchewan.

ANNE KEFFER (Lutheran) is Director of the Saskatchewan Centre for Ecumenism in Saskatoon, Saskatchewan.

ROBERT KELLY (Lutheran) is Professor of Systematic Theology at Waterloo Lutheran Seminary in Waterloo, Ontario.

RICHARD LEGGETT (Anglican) is Associate Professor of Liturgical Studies at Vancouver School of Theology in Vancouver, British Columbia.

MAYLANNE MAYBEE (Anglican) is Coordinator of Mission and Justice Education of the Anglican Church of Canada in Toronto, Ontario.

ROGER NOSTBAKKEN (Lutheran) is Emeritus Professor and sometime President of Lutheran Theological Seminary in Saskatoon, Saskatchewan.

RICHARD STETSON (Lutheran) is Assistant for Leadership for Ministry to the National Bishop of the Evangelical Lutheran Church in Canada in Winnipeg, Manitoba.

Abbreviations

BEM   *Baptism, Eucharist and Ministry.* Faith and Order Paper 111. Geneva: World Council of Churches, 1982.

CLAD I   Canadian Lutheran-Anglican Dialogue. *Report and Recommendations, April 1986.* Toronto, ON: Anglican Church of Canada, 1986; Winnipeg, MB: Evangelical Lutheran Church in Canada, 1986.

CLAD II   Canadian Lutheran-Anglican Dialogue. *Response to the Niagara Report.* Toronto, ON: Anglican Church of Canada, 1992; Winnipeg, MB: Evangelical Lutheran Church in Canada, 1992.

Hanover   *The Diaconate as Ecumenical Opportunity: The Hanover Report of the Anglican-Lutheran International Commission.* London, UK: Anglican Communion Publications, 1996.

Niagara   *The Niagara Report: Report of the Anglican-Lutheran Consultation on Episcope 1987.* London, UK: Church House Publishing, 1988.

Porvoo   *Together in Mission and Ministry: The Porvoo Common Statement with Essays on Church and Ministry in Northern Europe.* London, UK: Church House Publishing, 1993.

THE WATERLOO DECLARATION

(as approved by the Joint Working Group)

Draft
23 June 1997

Proposed text to be considered by
the National Convention of the Evangelical Lutheran Church in
Canada and the General Synod of the Anglican Church of Canada
Waterloo, Ontario
2001

Preface

1. In John 17.20–21, our Lord prayed that Christians might all be one so that the world might believe in Christ through the witness of our unity. The 20th century has given rise to an increase of movements which seek to give visible expression to this prayer. Christians have begun to see the fulfillment of Jesus' words as they unite in action to address the needs of local and global communities. The churches themselves have entered into partnerships at every level, from the neighbourhood to the world, through councils of churches, theological dialogues, and covenants which have fostered greater understanding in the search for common witness and visible unity. All these steps have moved us towards a healing of ancient divisions, including those which occurred during the 16th century in Europe.

2. Lutherans and Anglicans are graced in that we can respond to this prayer for unity without having experienced formal separation from one another. We share a common heritage as catholic churches of the

Reformation. Despite our previous geographic, linguistic and cultural differences, in recent years we have discovered in one another a shared faith and spirituality. This discovery has called us into a search for more visible unity in mission and ministry.

3. On the international scene, the Lutheran World Federation and the Anglican Consultative Council have participated in a number of formal discussions since 1972. These conversations were encouraged by the international multilateral consensus document *Baptism, Eucharist and Ministry* (Faith and Order Paper 111, WCC, 1982). In 1987, an international Lutheran-Anglican consultation on *episcope* was held in Niagara [Falls, Ontario]. From this gathering some specific recommendations were directed to the churches for their discussion. Consideration of these recommendations led in northern Europe to *The Porvoo Common Statement* (1993), and in the United States to the *Concordat of Agreement* (1997).

4. In 1983, Canadian Lutherans and Anglicans met to discuss the implications for the churches in Canada of the ongoing dialogue between Lutherans and Episcopalians in the United States. From this meeting emerged the Canadian Lutheran-Anglican Dialogue (CLAD), whose first series of meetings led to the publication of its *Report and Recommendations* (April, 1986). This report gave impetus to the desire of the two churches to produce an agreement which could provide a basis for the sharing of the eucharist between our churches.

5. A second series of discussion (CLAD II) resulted in the agreement *Interim Sharing of the Eucharist*, which was approved in 1989 by the National Convention of the Evangelical Lutheran Church in Canada and by the General Synod of the Anglican Church of Canada. In that agreement, we

i. agreed to live in a relationship of interim eucharistic sharing

ii. acknowledged one another as churches in which the Gospel is preached and taught

iii. committed ourselves to share a common life in mission and service, to pray for and with one another, and to share resources

6. The experience of six years of interim eucharistic sharing led the two churches in 1995 to take further steps towards full communion. The National Convention and the General Synod renewed the Interim Eucharistic Sharing Agreement until 2001 and further agreed

i. to request all neighbouring congregations to undertake joint projects and celebrate the eucharist together annually

ii. to receive one another's lay members, when moving from one church to the other with the same status (baptized/communicant/confirmed) which they held in their first church

iii. to foster the development and implementation of agreements which permit an ordained minister (priest or pastor) to serve the people of both churches, including presiding at the sacraments of the Church, wherever, and according to whichever rite, the local bishop of each church deems appropriate

iv. to develop structures with the purpose of evaluating and improving the bishop's ministry through collegial and periodic review

v. to call for our two churches to move towards full communion by 2001

7. Our two churches are using the following definition of full communion.

Full communion is understood as a relationship between two distinct churches or communions in which each maintains its own autonomy while recognizing the catholicity and apostolicity of the other, and believing the other to hold the essentials of the Christian faith. In such a relationship, communicant members of each church would be able freely to communicate at the altar of the other, and there would be freedom of ordained ministers to officiate sacramentally in either church. Specifically, in our context, we understand this to include transferability of members; mutual recognition and interchangeability of ministries; freedom to use each other's liturgies; freedom to participate in each other's ordinations and installations of clergy, including bishops; and structures for consultation to express, strengthen, and enable our common life, witness, and service, to the glory of God and the salvation of the world.

8. In a spirit of thanksgiving for what God has already accomplished in us, and with confidence and hope for what God has prepared for the whole Church, we believe we can now act in visible witness to the unity which is ours in Christ Jesus. We are taking the next step in our common pilgrimage of faith in the belief that it will be of service to a greater unity.

Proposed Joint Declaration

We, the Evangelical Lutheran Church in Canada and the Anglican Church of Canada, make the following acknowledgments and commitments.

A. Acknowledgments

1. We declare that in each church "the Gospel is preached in its purity and the holy sacraments are administered according to the Gospel" (Augsburg Confession VII), that in each church "the pure Word

of God is preached, and the Sacraments . . . duly administered according to Christ's ordinance in all those things that of necessity are requisite to the same." (Article XIX of *The Thirty-Nine Articles*)

2. We acknowledge that both our churches share in the common confession of the apostolic faith. (*Report and Recommendations, CLAD I, 1986*)

3. We acknowledge that personal, collegial and communal oversight (episcope) is embodied and exercised in both churches in a variety of forms, in continuity of apostolic life, mission and ministry. (*The Porvoo Common Statement, 1993*)

4. We acknowledge that the episcopal office is valued and maintained in both our churches as a visible sign expressing and serving the Church's unity and continuity in apostolic life, mission and ministry. (*The Porvoo Common Statement, 1993*)

5. We acknowledge that one another's ordained ministries are given by God as instruments of divine grace and as possessing not only the inward call of the Spirit, but also Christ's commission through his body, the Church (An Appeal to all Christian People, Lambeth Conference, 1920); and that these ministries are the gifts of God's Spirit to equip the people of God for the work of ministry. (Ephesians 4:11–12).

6. In the light of the above agreements, we make the following statements:

a. The Anglican Church of Canada hereby recognizes the full authenticity of the ordained ministries presently existing within the Evangelical Lutheran Church in Canada, acknowledging its pastors as priests in the Church of God and its bishops as chief pastors exercising a ministry of *episcope* over the jurisdictional areas of the Evangelical Lutheran Church in Canada in which they preside.

b. The Evangelical Lutheran Church in Canada hereby recognizes the full authenticity of the ordained ministries of bishops, priests, and deacons presently existing within the Anglican Church of Canada, acknowledging its priests as pastors in the Church of God and its bishops as chief pastors exercising a ministry of *episcope* over the jurisdictional areas of the Anglican Church of Canada in which they preside.

c. The Anglican Church of Canada and the Evangelical Lutheran Church in Canada each understands the bishops of both churches to be ordained for life service of the Gospel in the pastoral ministry of the historic episcopate, although tenure in office may be terminated by retirement, resignation or conclusion of term, subject to the constitutional provisions of the respective churches.

B. Declaration of Full Communion

We declare the Evangelical Lutheran Church in Canada and the Anglican Church of Canada to be in full communion.

C. Commitments

As churches in full communion, we now commit ourselves:

1. to welcome persons ordained in either of our churches to the office of bishop, priest/pastor or deacon to serve, by invitation and in accordance with any regulations which may from time to time be in force, in that ministry in the receiving church without re-ordination;

2. regularly to invite one another's bishops to participate in the laying on of hands at the ordination of bishops as a sign of the unity and continuity of the Church, and to invite pastors and priests to participate in the laying on of hands at the ordination of pastors or priests in each other's churches;

3. to work towards a common understanding of diaconal ministry;

4. to establish appropriate forms of collegial and conciliar consultation on significant matters of faith and order, mission and service;

5. to encourage regular consultation and collaboration among members of our churches at all levels, to promote the formulation and adoption of covenants for common work in mission and ministry, and to facilitate learning and exchange of ideas and information on theological, pastoral, and mission matters;

6. to establish a Joint Commission to nurture our growth in communion, to coordinate the implementation of this Declaration, and to report to the decision-making bodies of both our churches;

7. to hold joint meetings of national, regional and local decision-making bodies wherever practicable, and

8. to continue to work together for the full visible unity of the whole Church of God.

Conclusion

We rejoice in our Declaration as an expression of the visible unity of our churches in the one Body of Christ. We are ready to be co-workers with God in whatever tasks of mission serve the Gospel. We give glory to God for the gift of unity already ours in Christ, and we pray for the full realization of this gift in the entire Church.

(to be signed, if approved, by the National Bishop of the Evangelical Lutheran Church in Canada and the Primate of the Anglican Church of Canada)

Notes

Wording in sections A.2, 3, 4, 5; and C.1, 2, 3, 4, 5 is derived from *The Porvoo Common Statement* © David Tustin and Tore Furberg. Published in 1993 by Church House Publishing for the Council for Christian Unity of the General Synod of the Church of England.

Wording in section A.6 is derived from *Concordat of Agreement* between the Episcopal Church and the Evangelical Lutheran Church in America, revised January 1997, published for study by the Office of Ecumenical Relations of the Episcopal Church.

COMMENTARY ON THE
WATERLOO DECLARATION
as approved by the Joint Working Group,
November 1, 1998[1]

A. Acknowledgements

1. We understand the Anglican and Lutheran churches to be catholic churches of the Reformation. We are catholic in that we have remained faithful to the apostolic teaching and fellowship as expressed in the canonical scriptures of the Old and New Testaments and in the Apostles' and Nicene Creeds. We celebrate the sacraments of our redemption, baptism, and eucharist, and maintain a historic continuity in office of those exercising the apostolic commission.

We are churches of the Reformation in that we share the common experience of renewal and revisioning that we know as the Reformation of the sixteenth and seventeenth centuries. This experience has led both our churches to root our faith in the sufficiency of God's grace freely given to the believer. This faith finds expression in works of love which spring from a trust and reliance in God's providential care for us and for the whole created order.

Agreement in the gospel is fundamental to full communion between our churches. We believe and proclaim the gospel: that in Christ God has reconciled the world to God's very self and that for anyone who is in Christ there is a new creation. Through the Holy Spirit we are given power to become children of God and to grow into the full stature of Christ.

---

1 The members of the Joint Working Group acknowledge their debt to Roger Nostbakken, who prepared the initial draft of this commentary for the consideration of the group.

We understand the Church as the communion of saints in which the gospel is purely taught and preached and the sacraments are administered according to the gospel and Christ's ordinance. The liturgy proclaims the gospel as a celebration of salvation through Christ under the forms of water, bread, and wine. In baptism we are made members of the community of the Church. In the holy communion we are nourished spiritually and our unity with Christ and with each other is strengthened. In receiving Christ in the eucharist we receive the forgiveness of sins, are reconciled to God and each other, are nurtured in the communion of saints, are given power in love and service, and receive hope in the foretaste of the feast to come.

2. Our churches share a common faith. This is expressed in mutual acceptance of the canonical scriptures of the Old and New Testaments and the Nicene-Constantinopolitan and Apostles' Creeds. We use similar orders of service and see in the liturgy both celebration of salvation and actualization of the *consensus fidelium* ("the mind of the Church, lay and ordained"). As members of the community of faith, our churches seek to submit to Jesus Christ in the teaching, mission, and ministry of the whole Church. This is expressed in the doctrine of apostolicity.

Apostolicity means continuity in the permanent characteristics of the Church of the apostles. As God's gift in Christ through the Holy Spirit, apostolicity is not confined to the historic episcopate but is a diverse reality expressed in the church's teaching, mission, and ministry. Apostolic teaching is expressed not only in the scriptures and historic ecumenical creeds but also in the confessional documents developed at the time of the Reformation. The particular confessions of our churches are seen as further witnesses of the faith of the Church catholic by being expositions of the Holy Scriptures. The similar tradition of liturgical worship in our churches is further witness to a common faith and understanding of the Church.

The apostolic mission of the Church is rooted in the sending of Christ in the power of the Spirit into the world by the Father, and in the sending of the apostles by Christ in the power of that same Spirit. This latter sending is shared by all members of the Church. Within the Church varieties of ministries are conferred by the Holy Spirit in the service of apostolic mission.

3. The ministry of *episcope* is a ministry of leadership bearing the authority of Christ in and to the community and involves fidelity to the apostolic faith, its proclamation, and its transmission to future generations. This ministry of oversight is a caring for the life of the whole community, a pastoring of the pastors, and a true feeding of the whole of Christ's flock. *Episcope* is entrusted to the whole Church and is exercised in the light of the gospel.

The ministry of oversight is the particular responsibility of the bishop whose office is one of service and communication within the community of faith. Bishops preach the word, preside at sacraments, and administer discipline in the service of oversight, continuity, and unity. This ministry of pastoral oversight serves the apostolicity, catholicity, and unity of the Church's teaching, mission, and sacramental life. None of this is done in isolation from the whole Church, but the ministry of oversight is exercised personally, collegially, and communally. As a personal ministry, *episcope* points to the presence of Christ by proclaiming the gospel and calling the community to serve in unity of life and witness. *Episcope* is collegial in that the bishop gathers those ordained to the tasks of ministry and takes counsel with them to determine how best to enable the ministry and mission of the whole Church. It is collegial also in that the collegiality of bishops locally relates to the wider Church. It is communal because ordained ministry is rooted in the life of the community and requires the community's effective participation. The personal, collegial, and communal aspects of oversight find expression at all levels of the Church's life.

4. The episcopal office is a visible and personal sign of the apostolicity of the whole Church. This is grounded in the promise of Christ and the presence of the Holy Spirit at work in the whole Church. Succession in the episcopal office provides continuity of the apostolic life and mission of the Church through the ministry of oversight. Continuity in episcopal succession is signified in the ordination of a bishop. Through the laying on of hands the whole Church calls on God to pour out the Holy Spirit on his people.

Through ordination to episcopal office the Church communicates its care for continuity in the whole of its life and mission. In the service of ordination a public declaration of the faith of the Church and an expression of episcopal ministry help to make clear the meaning of the office as such a sign of continuity. This sign does not guarantee the faithfulness of the Church to its faith, life, and mission, nor does it guarantee the personal fidelity of the bishop. It is nonetheless witness to continuity of proclamation of the gospel of Christ and the mission of his Church.

Faithfulness to the apostolic calling of the whole Church is maintained by more than one means of continuity. These means include "witness to the apostolic faith, proclamation and fresh interpretation of the Gospel, celebration of baptism and the eucharist, the transmission of ministerial responsibilities, communion in prayer, love, joy and suffering, service to the sick and needy, unity among the local churches and sharing the gifts which the Lord has given to each."[2] In the light of this understanding of the signs of continuity, we recognize that the substance of *episcope* is present in both our churches, although the exercise of *episcope* has taken different shapes. The resumption of the sign of an ordained episcopate is not an adverse judgement on the past; it is a means of making more visible the unity and continuity of the Church at all times and in all places. By the sharing of our life and ministries in closer visible unity our churches are strengthened for the continuation of Christ's mission in the world.

5. We believe all members of the Church are called to participate in its apostolic mission through a variety of ministries. Ordained ministry exists to serve the ministry of the whole people of God.

"[Our churches] acknowledge ordained ministry to be a gift of God to the Church, and thus of divine institution ... Ordination is an act of Christ in the Church" (*CLAD I*, "Agreed Statement on Ordained Ministry," paragraphs 25, 26). In the name of the Church and in the power of the Holy Spirit, those who are authorized to ordain do so with the laying on of hands and with the prayer of the whole assembly.

Ordained ministry is regarded by our churches as essential for the Church and is exercised as a public office. For this reason the oversight of pastoral ministry through the office of *episcope* is seen as fundamental to the life, unity, and mission of the Church.

---

2 *BEM*, "Ministry," paragraph 34.

As joint heirs of the catholic tradition both our churches share a common basic understanding of the place of ordained ministry in the Church. Ordained ministry signifies the essential dimensions of the ministry entrusted by Christ to the Church and exercised by both of our churches.

It has been possible therefore for our churches to acknowledge each other as churches where the gospel is truly preached and taught and the sacraments are rightly administered. It is further possible to affirm one another as churches that possess a genuine and authentic ministry of Word and Sacrament which derives from the teaching of the apostles and the practice of the early church.

6. In view of the substantive agreements between our churches on all matters fundamental to faith and ministry, it has become possible for us to make statements of mutual recognition of ordained ministry and episcopal oversight.

> a. The Anglican Church of Canada recognizes the authenticity of ordered ministries in the Evangelical Lutheran Church in Canada including both the offices of pastor and of bishop.

> b. The Evangelical Lutheran Church in Canada recognizes the authenticity of ordered ministries in the Anglican Church of Canada including the offices of deacon, priest, and bishop.

> c. Our respective histories have caused our two churches to view somewhat differently the office of the historic episcopate. Anglicans have traditionally focused on the office as a sign of apostolic teaching, ministry, and mission. The Lutheran Confessions have focused on the office as meaningful primarily as it contributes to the unity of the Church in faith and witness to the universality of the gospel of reconciliation. Both of these understandings come together in our present acknowledgements and agreements.

Both our churches understand and accept the office of bishop to be that of *episcope*. Each church further understands that bishops are ordained for life service in the ministry of the historic episcopate. At the same time it is acknowledged that episcopal tenure is subject to termination by retirement, resignation, conclusion of term, or removal for cause as provided in the respective constitutions of our churches.

B. Declaration of Full Communion

The declaration of full communion between our churches is a step of enormous historic significance and millennial promise. Our two churches have existed for centuries sharing a common heritage as catholic churches of the Reformation, but living separately and parallel. We now come together in a visible witness to the unity which is ours in Jesus Christ. Full communion is not an organic union or merger of our churches but is a relationship of fundamental unity. Each church retains its autonomy of decision and governance, while at the same time recognizes and affirms each other's catholicity and apostolicity, and acknowledges the authenticity of one another's faith and doctrine.

A declaration of full communion is an acknowledgement of mutual trust, confidence, and respect. In this relationship communicant members of each church are free to communicate at each other's altars and ordained clergy are eligible to preside at the celebration of the sacraments in either church. Full communion also makes possible transferability of members, interchangeability of ordained ministries, and use of each other's liturgies. Ordination and installation of clergy including bishops are open to participation by each other's clergy and bishops.

This declaration also implies mutuality in consultative structures intended to express, strengthen, and enable common life, witness, and service in all aspects of the life and mission of the Church.

C. Commitments

Full communion means not only recognition and acknowledgement and mutually acceptable statements but also a commitment to live out actively in day to day experience the implications of that communion. These implications include specific commitments.

1. We have come to trust the integrity of each church in its process of calling and preparing candidates for the ministry of Word and Sacrament. Both of our churches are agreed that ordination can be received only once and is not a repeatable act. We are also in agreement that the essential and specific function of the ordained ministry is to gather and build up the Christian community by proclaiming the Word of God, celebrating the sacraments, and presiding over the liturgical, diaconal, and missionary life of the community. We therefore commit ourselves to welcome the clergy of either church to exercise their ministries in either church subject to appropriate regulation.

2. Each of our churches is committed to inviting one another's bishops to participate in the laying on of hands at episcopal ordinations, and to inviting pastors and priests to participate in the laying on of hands at pastoral or priestly ordinations. It is our expectation that, as churches in full communion, bishops from both churches will normally participate in every episcopal ordination. This commitment is an expression of our churches' recognition of episcopal succession as a visible sign of the churches' unity and continuity in apostolic life, mission, and ministry.

We have come to acknowledge the present apostolic reality of the existing ordained ministries of our churches. This mutual acknowledgement of our churches and ministries precedes the use of the sign of the laying on of hands in the historic succession. Consequently, resumption of the use of the sign by Lutherans does not imply an adverse judgement on a ministry which did not previously make use of the sign, but is rather a vivid expression of the Evangelical Lutheran Church in Canada's commitment to the visible unity of the whole Church.

Likewise, the Anglican Church of Canada commits itself to full communion with the Evangelical Lutheran Church in Canada on the basis of a renewed understanding of the relationship of the historic episcopate and apostolicity.[3] This is not an abandonment on the part of Anglicans of their heritage. Rather, Anglicans have come to recognize in the ministries of the Evangelical Lutheran Church in Canada

---

3 *BEM*, "Ministry," paragrahs 34–38; *Niagara*, paragraphs 20–24, 29–30, 48–49, 52–59, 68–69, 71, 73; *Porvoo*, paragraphs 34–57.

that apostolicity which Anglicans have experienced in the threefold ministry of bishops, priests, and deacons.

3. Both our churches acknowledge *diakonia* has a place within the ministerial office and are therefore committed to the continuing study and reform which will ensure a common understanding of diaconal ministry. Such study will include its place within the ministerial office and its relationship with other ministries.

4. Our churches commit themselves to establish forms of collegial and conciliar consultations on all significant matters and at every stage in the development of this new relationship. The establishment of full communion compels us to consider questions of doctrine, worship, and discipline together. We will travel on a common pilgrimage, side by side, rather than on individual paths that occasionally intersect.

5. Our churches commit themselves to regular consultation and collaboration on all significant matters and at every stage in the development of this new relationship. This commitment may lead us, for example, to consider having representatives of one church on appropriate commissions, committees, and boards of the other church. Such considerations are the natural outcome since full communion is intended to lead us into deeper unity.

6. To assist in planning for mission, to nourish our growth in communion, and to coordinate the implementation of this declaration, a joint commission will be established by and be accountable to both churches. The purpose of the joint commission will be to facilitate consultation and common decision-making through appropriate channels in fundamental matters faced by our churches. Although the agenda of the joint commission will be open to direction by the churches, it might include such matters as the appropriate regulations for receiving clergy from each other's churches, ensuring the participation of each other's clergy in ordinations, developing a common understanding of diaconal ministry, and developing appropriate

structures for consultation and collaboration in theological, pastoral, and mission matters.

7. Our churches also commit themselves to hold joint meetings of national, regional, and local decision-making bodies wherever practicable and useful This will be an embodiment of the life of full communion and an expression of joint ministry and mission.

8. Joint meetings and cooperative ventures represent a commitment to making visible in the day to day life of our churches the full visible unity of the whole Church of God. The churches are permanently committed to common mission and ministry, recognizing each other fully as churches in which the gospel is preached and the holy sacraments administered.

Each church will continue to live in communion with all the churches with whom they are now in communion. This does not imply or inaugurate any automatic communion beyond these present arrangements.

Both our churches will continue their dialogues with other churches and traditions. Where appropriate, both churches will seek to engage in joint dialogues. On the basis of the Declaration of Full Communion, both churches are committed to prior consultation before entering into formal agreements with other churches and traditions. At the same time such commitments are in no way intended to impede the development of relationships and agreements with other churches and traditions with whom they have been in dialogue.

Conclusion

Both churches recognize that unity is both our Lord's prayer for us (John 17) and a gift already given to us by God in Christ (Ephesians 4.1–6). We have been entrusted with the task of making this unity even more visible.

Full communion between Lutherans and Anglicans in Canada marks but one step toward the eventual visible unity of the whole Church catholic. We have entered a new stage on our journey together; there may yet be stages that we can only imagine dimly at this point. Nevertheless, we give glory to God whose power, working in us, can do infinitely more than we can ask or imagine. Glory to God from generation to generation, in the Church and in Christ Jesus, for ever and ever. Amen (Ephesians 3.20–21).

FROM WITTENBERG TO WATERLOO:
A Sketch of Canadian Lutheranism

Robert A. Kelly

THE BEGINNING OF THE Lutheran Reformation is credited to a debate among university theological professors on questions related to the practice of penance. Perhaps, then, it should not be a surprise that the Reformation in Germany and Scandinavia centred on theological questions in which the forgiveness of sins played a primary role. Certainly there were reforms of worship orders and church governance, but these were carried out differently in different territories and were not an issue of contention among the Lutheran reformers.

The Lutheran Reformation was also more influenced by a particular person than perhaps other parts of the Reformation. Martin Luther not only gave his name to the movement, but also, after the scriptures and the ecumenical creeds, is the most significant theological influence on Lutheranism. Luther's concern was that the church had drifted away from recognizing the crucified Jesus as its Lord and had become more concerned about promoting human achievement and its own glory. He believed that the biblical gospel of God's freely-given grace was being contradicted by teachings about what human beings must do in order to merit God's favour — "good works."[1] He

---

1 We should note that the sixteenth-century disputes on the doctrine of justification between the Lutheran church and the Roman Catholic Church are well on their way to resolution in the present. The *Joint Declaration on the Doctrine of Justification 1997* has been prepared and was endorsed by the 1997 Assembly of the Lutheran World Federation. This declaration was based on

also believed that the preaching of the gospel of justification by grace through faith would have the power in and of itself to reform the various abuses and corruptions in the late-medieval church. Lutherans originally called themselves "Evangelicals" because of this emphasis on the gospel. Lutherans refer to themselves as a "reform movement in the Church catholic" or as "Evangelical Catholics."

In the early years the goal of the Lutheran movement was to reform the Church catholic through teaching, preaching, and celebrating the sacraments. Changes in liturgy and church governance came slowly. Preaching on scripture in the vernacular was emphasized and the number of weekday services was reduced to two. The mass was made less complicated, but remained mostly in Latin (except for sermon and hymns) until Christmas 1525. There was also a reluctance to ordain pastors or reorganize the parishes until it became obvious that no bishop in Germany would ever ordain anyone who held Lutheran sympathies and would take no responsibility for parishes in territories where the Reformation was adopted. Finally in 1528–1529 the situation of rural parishes was so desperate that the Elector of Saxony ordered the reorganization of parishes in his territories, an action followed by other rulers who had adopted the Reformation. This date really marks the beginning of "Lutheran" churches, though these churches were generally called by the name of the territory. As part of this reorganization, Luther produced his *Small Catechism* for the instruction of the laity in the fundamentals of the Christian faith. This little book has remained at the heart of Lutheran piety and teaching ever since.

In 1530 the Holy Roman Emperor, Charles V, who was an ardent opponent of the Reformation, called the Lutheran principalities and cities to give account of themselves and their teaching at the imperial diet, held in Augsburg. The leaders of the Lutheran territories appointed Philip Melanchthon, Luther's colleague and the second most

---

the work of a variety of Lutheran-Roman Catholic dialogue groups and will be signed by representatives of the Lutheran World Federation and the Vatican on October 31, 1999. In paragraph 40, this declaration states, "The understanding of the doctrine of justification set forth in the Declaration shows that a consensus in basic truths of the doctrine of justification exists between Lutherans and Catholics."

influential Lutheran theologian, to produce a confession of faith which would both state the basic teachings of the Lutherans and draw attention to the abuses against which they were protesting. This document became known as the *Augsburg Confession* and is the fundamental defining document of Lutheran teaching. Among Lutherans, the *Small Catechism* and the *Augsburg Confession* are seen as faithful interpretations of the Holy Scriptures and the ecumenical creeds, and continue to play an important role in the church.

From Germany the Lutheran Reformation spread to Denmark (which at that time included Norway), Sweden (including Finland), the Baltic territories, some communities in Bohemia and Moravia, and Transylvania. As in Germany, the Lutheran Reformation tended to be a conservative reform movement, changing only what was necessary to secure the preaching of the gospel of justification by grace and the celebration of the sacraments in a manner that communicated grace rather than human works. Each territorial or national church produced its own orders of worship and system of governance. Most of the orders of worship were similar and were also quite similar to the orders used in the *Book of Common Prayer* in England. There was more variety in the systems of governance, with the secular rulers usually being the ultimate authority as in England.

A series of wars was fought in the 1540s and 1550s. The *Peace of Augsburg* in 1555 secured the right of territories in the Holy Roman Empire to remain Lutheran. This peace did not last and war broke out again in 1618. The *Peace of Westphalia* in 1648 finally brought the end of religious wars to the empire and guaranteed that Lutherans would not be denied the right to practise their faith. The many years of warfare had taken their toll on the German people and the church was in desperate need of renewal. This renewal came from a movement that came to be called "Pietism," which began in southern Germany in the latter seventeenth century and spread from there. Pietism was quite influential in Germany in the eighteenth century, where it led to an upsurge in interest in social welfare, and in Scandinavia in the nineteenth century, particularly Norway, where it was part of the movement for Norwegian independence. Lutheran pietism also had some influence in England on both the Wesleyan movement (through contacts between John Wesley and the Moravians) and the Anglican

Evangelical movement (through the influence of the royal family after the Duke of Hanover became George I).

As the influence of the Pietist movement waned in Germany, rationalism led the church into a period of decline. In the early nineteenth century the King of Prussia decided that the Lutheran and Reformed churches in his dominion ought to be united into one, the Church of the Prussian Union. The king also produced a new liturgy, which was imposed on the church. This led to a renewal movement among Lutherans not only in Prussia and her territories, but throughout Germany. Scholars once again studied Luther and Melanchthon. The theology of the Reformation was revived. Liturgical studies brought renewal and a return to historic forms. A stronger sense of the church developed. This "Confessional Revival," akin to the Oxford Movement in England, helped shape both the European and North American Lutheran churches during the nineteenth and into the twentieth century. It also influenced the development of other younger Lutheran churches that were growing up in Africa, Asia, and Oceania.

Lutheranism in North America has always led a somewhat enigmatic existence. On the one hand, Lutheran worship services have been held on this continent as early as the winter of 1620 when a Danish expedition attempting to find the Northwest Passage spent the winter near present-day Churchill, Manitoba. At the same time, Lutheran history in North America is especially marked by the fact that Lutherans came here as immigrants who did not speak English, always just outside the Anglophone mainstream.

Permanent settlement of Lutherans can be dated to New Sweden. After the American Revolution the archbishop of Uppsala refused to send pastors and the Swedish congregations became part of the Episcopal Church, so the oldest continuing Lutheran congregations in North America are those founded in New Amsterdam in 1649 and Albany in 1669. The earliest Lutherans to immigrate to Canada arrived in Halifax in 1750. They established St. George's, now a parish of the Anglican Church of Canada. The oldest continuing Lutheran congregation in Canada is Zion Church in Lunenburg, Nova Scotia. From the 1790s, Lutheran Loyalists settled in the St. Lawrence Valley and north of Toronto. Beginning in the 1830s they were joined by immigrants directly from Germany. As the nineteenth century progressed, the immigration from Germany increased and the Germans were joined by Danes, Swedes, Norwegians, Finns, and Icelanders. For almost all of these immigrant communities the primary problem was securing qualified pastors. Since in many European countries the clergy occupied a privileged position, many were reluctant to accept the frontier conditions under which most of the immigrants lived. In the eighteenth century the University of Halle, the centre of the German Pietist movement, supplied the majority of clergy for North American congregations. One of these, Henry Melchior Muhlenberg, organized the congregations of Pennsylvania into a synod known as the Pennsylvania Ministerium. The ministerium produced church orders and liturgies, which became widely used in the new world. Muhlenberg also brought some regularity to the training of indigenous clergy for the North American congregations. This eventually led to the establishment of the first North American Lutheran seminary at Gettysburg, Pennsylvania, in 1820.

The shortage of clergy continued among the most recent immigrants until the very end of the nineteenth century. As a result, congregations tended to identify with whichever synod could supply them with a pastor. Particularly in Canada qualified pastors continued to be in short supply, since almost all came from either Europe or the United States. Congregations begged sister synods in the United States to send pastors, but few responded. Finally in 1911, the Canada Synod (German-speaking) and the Synod of Central Canada (English-speaking) established Waterloo Lutheran Seminary in order to educate Canadians for the Lutheran ministry. A German and a Norwegian seminary were also established in Saskatoon to supply the need in western Canada. These two seminaries later merged to become Lutheran Theological Seminary.

One result of the patterns of immigration was that Lutherans were scattered and split by linguistic and geographic divisions. Theological controversies in nineteenth-century Europe added to the division. Because Lutherans came from a variety of national and regional churches in Europe, there was no single authority which could bring unity. German Lutherans maintained ties with their home provincial churches or with whichever university or missionary society would supply pastors. Scandinavians looked to their respective national churches. Old rivalries from Europe, different languages, and different traditions in liturgy and polity made unity difficult in the new world. Yet Lutherans in North America also came from a tradition in which there was a single Lutheran church in each nation or territory. The unity of the church was an important value. Beginning with the 400th Anniversary of the Reformation in 1917, Lutherans began the hard work of overcoming division. Two major mergers in that year began the trend toward Lutheran unity which culminated in 1986 with the formation of the Evangelical Lutheran Church in Canada (ELCIC) and in 1988 with the formation of the Evangelical Lutheran Church in America (ELCA). One major Lutheran body remains outside of this quest for unity, the Lutheran Church–Missouri Synod, and its Canadian counterpart, the Lutheran Church–Canada. North American Lutherans have also been active in the Ecumenical Movement of the twentieth century, serving in the formation of the World Council of Churches, the National Council of Churches in the US, and the Canadian Council of Churches. Lutherans in Canada have given time and effort to the ecumenical social justice coalitions. Through the Lutheran World Federation and national and regional bodies, Lutherans have been eager participants in bilateral dialogues seeking to heal the divisions of the past.

Throughout Lutheran history in North America, assimilation to the Anglophone mainstream has been an issue. In the 1830s, '40s, and '50s a debate raged among English-speaking American Lutherans. This debate died down as more and more immigrants arrived from Europe who, for the first two generations, had little interest in the issues. Again, by 1914 there were many Lutherans who were primarily English-speaking, but the wave of prejudice against German-Americans and German-Canadians during World War I kept the issues from being addressed. Since the 1960s Lutherans once again have had the opportunity to assimilate into the Anglophone mainstream, but questions have arisen. As in the early nineteenth century, some Lutherans believe that the best future for Lutherans would be to become a mainline Protestant church. Others believe that Lutherans ought to emphasize the catholic parts of the Lutheran heritage and avoid the Protestant mainstream. Still others believe that Lutherans ought to emphasize church growth and become more like Evangelical Protestants.

In spite of whatever controversy exists, most Lutherans are committed to being Lutherans, that is, to being Christian people who believe deeply that God justifies all people in Christ by grace alone, through faith alone, and who also believe deeply in the unity of the church. As in the sixteenth century, so today, Lutherans desire to be Evangelical Catholics, a confessing movement that calls the whole Church to celebrate and live in the grace of God in Christ.

A REVIEW OF ANGLICAN–LUTHERAN DIALOGUES

John Flynn

(1) The Reformation of the Sixteenth Century

Anglicans and Lutherans share common roots both in the patristic and medieval church and in the Reformation of the sixteenth century. Despite this fact, their relationship with one another has unfolded slowly, moving from separate development to significant though not full communion, to the present situation in which the question of full communion is being actively pursued. A word needs to be said about all three of these stages.

The Reformation itself was not a single event, but a series of events spread out over a period of eighty or more years. These events gave rise not to a single Protestant church but, broadly speaking, to four families of churches, each of which saw itself as a return to the doctrine and practice of the apostolic age. Each faced two basic tasks: (a) to break with "corrupt" teaching, practices, and structures of the late medieval church and (b) to enact the establishment (or, as the reformers thought of it, the "re-establishment") of scripturally appropriate doctrine, practices, and structures for the future. Both of these tasks were executed in widely divergent social and political contexts and both took a considerable period of time.

The Lutheran Reformation may be said to have formally begun in 1522 with the condemnation of Martin Luther at the Diet of Worms.[1] That condemnation was the outcome of the attack initiated

---

1 The diet was the legislative body of the Holy Roman Empire which met at a variety of locations.

by Luther in 1517 on the indulgences being preached in Germany to raise money for the rebuilding of St. Peter's basilica in Rome. The principal Lutheran confessional document, the *Augsburg Confession*, did not see the light of day until 1530 and the authoritative collection of the key Lutheran confessional documents was not completed until the *Formula of Concord* in 1577.

At almost the same time as events in Germany, a second and independent strand of the Protestant Reformation began in Switzerland and the Rhineland. Led by theologians such as Ulrich Zwingli, this second strand came to be associated more closely with the name of John Calvin and is more properly called the Reformed tradition. Key figures of this tradition include Heinrich Bullinger, Martin Bucer, and Peter Martyr Vermigli. These three theologians also influenced the reformation of the Church in England, and both Vermigli and Bucer taught in England during the reign of Edward VI. The earliest confessional statement from the Reformed tradition was Zwingli's *Sixty-Seven Articles* of 1523. Bullinger's *Second Helvetic Confession* did not appear until 1566 and the famous *Westminster Confession* was not completed until 1646.

The third movement is the so-called "Anabaptist" movement. This term was originally a term of abuse and the tradition is better known as the Radical Reformation. Its influence on the other three movements was largely negative in character. Its leaders were many, among the better known of whom were Thomas Müntzer, Jacob Hutter, and Menno Simons.

The English Reformation constitutes the fourth movement. It was energized by what was happening on the continent but motivated and shaped by distinctively English needs. Although Henry VIII was responsible for the break with Rome, the enduring shape of the settlement did not occur until the reign of Elizabeth I. The issue of further reform was not put to rest finally until the restoration of Charles II to the throne of England in 1660 after the period of the Commonwealth.

Once Henry VIII had broken with Rome, theological conversations with the German Lutherans became acceptable. At least one of these conversations had direct influence on the doctrinal shape of the English Reformation. This occurred as the indirect result of a conference held in London in 1536. Although Henry lost interest in subsequent conversations, a draft of *Thirteen Articles* survived the conference and was later found in the papers of Thomas Cranmer. These articles contain a number of direct citations from the *Augsburg Confession* (1530) and had a direct impact on the text of the *Forty-Two Articles of Religion* drafted by Cranmer in 1553. When these articles were revised in 1563 and became the *Thirty-Nine Articles of Religion*, these citations were retained and reference was also made to another Lutheran confession, the *Württemburg Confession* of 1552.

(2) From the Seventeenth Century to the Twentieth Century

Anglican-Lutheran relations did not flourish in the seventeenth century but neither was contact entirely broken. When a new Danish church was built in London in 1692, the residents of that city were surprised to discover that the Danish pastor wore eucharistic vestments, something the English regarded as "popish."

Somewhat better relations occurred in the New World. The Swedes had established a colony at Wilmington on the Delaware River in 1637. The colony was conquered by the Dutch in 1655 and in turn the Dutch were conquered by the English in 1664. Almost all of the Swedish churches and their ministers were gradually absorbed into the Church of England. When, after the American Revolution, the Protestant Episcopal Church was being organized, the question of how to secure ordination for its priests and bishops became an issue. Initially, the English bishops could not ordain the American candidates because of English statute law requiring the bishops to obtain an oath of allegiance to the Crown from every ordinand. Some thought was given to the possibility of having candidates for the priesthood ordained by Danish Lutheran bishops and apparently an offer was received from the Church of Sweden to provide episcopal consecration. This became unnecessary when Samuel Seabury was consecrated bishop by the bishops of the Scottish Episcopal Church in 1784 and Parliament altered statute law to permit the consecration of three bishops for the American church. But it was in what came to be called "the foreign missions" that Anglican-Lutheran relations were most productive. From 1710 to 1725 the Society for Promoting Christian Knowledge (SPCK) gave financial support to the Danish Lutheran Mission in Tranquebar, India. Sixty Lutheran pastors were directly employed by SPCK from 1728 to 1825 to serve its own mission in India, numbering among them Christian Friedrich Schwartz, who served from 1750 until his death in 1798.

India was not the only place where Lutheran-Anglican cooperation occurred. A British colony had been established in Sierra Leone in 1792 by transporting one thousand free Afro-Canadians from Nova Scotia. When Anglican clergy could not be secured for the colony, the Society for Missions to Africa and the East (later known as the Church Mission Society [CMS]) recruited two German Lutherans in 1804 and another three in 1806. This policy remained in force for a decade. In 1817 the London officers of the society advised their best lay missionary in Sierra Leone, one W. A. B. Johnson, to seek ordination from the society's Lutheran missioners in the colony. The ordination took place on 31 March 1817. No Anglican bishop was forthcoming for Sierra Leone until the consecration of Owen Vidal in 1852.

A more infamous example was the sanction by the British and Prussian governments of a "Protestant bishop in Jerusalem." Both governments saw the move as a way to increase their political influence in the area and to counter that of France on behalf of Roman Catholics and that of Russia on behalf of the Orthodox. The governmental agreement called for Prussia and Great Britain each to provide one-half of the bishop's salary. The bishop was to be nominated alternately by the respective sovereigns and to be consecrated by English bishops. The agreement soon became a dead letter and no Prussian ever held the office. The bishopric exists to this day as the Diocese of Jerusalem in the Anglican Province of Jerusalem and the Middle East.

(3) Twentieth-Century Dialogue

(a) From Occasional Cooperation to Dialogue

A second phase in Anglican-Lutheran relations unfolded in the period from 1867 to 1987. It was one of dialogue and movement toward significant though not yet full communion. This phase developed in three movements: (i) Britain and Scandinavia, (ii) Africa and Asia, and (iii) intensive dialogue and interim forms of fellowship or communion.

(i) Britain and Scandinavia

Initially the focus was on relations between the Church of England and the Church of Sweden. While preparations were underway for the first Lambeth Conference in 1867, the Rev. Charles Kingsley wrote to the archbishop of Canterbury, urging him to include the bishops of the Church of Sweden in the list of those invited. Though this did not come to pass, a seed had been planted. An initiative from the Church of Sweden caused the 1888 Lambeth Conference to applaud the " . . . approaches on the part of the Swedish Church with a view to the mutual explanation of differences . . . in order to the ultimate establishment, if possible, of intercommunion on solid principles of ecclesiastical polity" (*Resolution 14*). At the next Lambeth Conference (1897), the archbishop of Canterbury was asked to appoint a commission on behalf of the Anglican Communion to inquire into certain questions dealing with ordinations in the Swedish church; the commission was to report back to the following Lambeth Conference (1908). The inquiry had not reached a conclusion by that time and the 1908 conference authorized an extension to the commission's mandate (*Resolution 74*).

The official report appeared in 1911. The commission reported its opinion that the succession of bishops had been maintained unbroken by the Swedish church and that there was a true conception of the episcopal office. Further, the commission stated that the office of priest was rightly understood to be a divinely-instituted instrument for the ministry of Word and Sacraments and that this understanding had been maintained throughout the history of the Swedish church.

It should be noted here that the report acknowledged the statement of the Swedish bishops that they did not regard the possession of the historic episcopate as a necessary condition for full communion. The report further recommended that members of the Swedish church otherwise qualified to receive communion in that church be admitted to communion in Anglican churches and that Swedish clergy be permitted to preach in parishes of the Church of England.

Communion-wide reaction to the report was delayed by the advent of World War I. The next Lambeth Conference was not held until 1920. That conference, however, asked that the recommendations of the report be adopted by the various autonomous provinces of the Anglican Communion. At the same time it authorized the participation of Anglican bishops in the consecration of Swedish bishops, if invited to do so (*Resolution 24*). The invitation was forthcoming and two Anglican bishops participated in the consecration of two Swedish bishops at Uppsala on 19 September 1920. On 1 November 1927 a Swedish bishop participated in the consecration of three Anglican bishops at Canterbury. This practice was interrupted from 1959 to sometime after 1976 because of the decision of the Swedish church to ordain woman pastors.

Discussions with the Finnish church were held between 1933 and 1934, but political conditions delayed the first Anglican participation in the consecration of a Finnish bishop until 1951. The Baltic churches of Estonia and Latvia also held discussions with the Church of England in 1936 and 1938. The Second World War and the Soviet occupation delayed Anglican participation in a Baltic consecration until 1989.

(ii) Africa and Asia

The second movement unfolded in what we today often call the "Third World." On the Indian subcontinent Anglicans, Congregationalists, Presbyterians, and Methodists entered into a dialogue which led to the formation of the Church of South India (CSI) in 1947. Thereafter, Lutherans joined in discussions about church unity, particularly in the 1970s, in both parts of India as well as Pakistan. Only in Pakistan, however, did Anglicans and Lutherans both enter a united church. The CSI, about one-half of whose members had formerly been

Anglicans, held extensive discussions with various Lutheran churches during the 1950s and 1960s. Matters went as far as the preparation of a constitution of a new Church of Christ in South India, but the issue never came to a vote.

A similar tale may be told of Africa: much discussion but, in the end, disappointment. The most elaborate conversations were held in Ghana in the 1960s and in Zimbabwe in the 1970s. Perhaps the most significant encounter between Lutheran and Anglicans in Africa occurred during the course of the East Africa Church Union Consultation in the 1960s. After very lengthy discussions in Dodoma in 1965 a stalemate was reached. The overt issue was that of episcopacy, but a number of other tensions, political in nature, were also at work. Still, the conversations were not without fruit. They produced the *East Africa United Liturgy* which is still used today, with very minor verbal changes, in both Anglican and Lutheran churches in Tanzania. Relations between the two communions in Tanzania have continued to be cordial. Indeed, Anglican and Lutheran bishops regularly participate in each other's consecrations, including the laying on of hands. An example of this was the consecration of Basil Sambano as the Anglican bishop of Dar es Salaam in 1992.

(iii) Intensive Dialogue and Interim Forms of Fellowship or Communion

The third movement began in the 1960s. This process was undoubtedly helped by the establishment of the Anglican Consultative Council (ACC) as a parallel organization to the Lutheran World Federation (LWF). The announcement by Pope John XXIII of the Second Vatican Council also had a favourable impact on Anglican-Lutheran relations. In 1963 the Commission on World Mission of the LWF suggested that a study committee to prepare for worldwide Anglican-Lutheran conversations be authorized. The LWF's Commission on Theology endorsed the request that same year and a number of quiet contacts were initiated. These contacts led to the formation of an ad-hoc committee which met in Berlin in November 1967. This committee in turn proposed that the approaching Lambeth Conference and the executive of the LWF authorize a "representative Anglican-Lutheran Commission." Significantly, when the 1968 Lambeth

Conference endorsed this suggestion, one of the supporting reasons given was the accelerating pace of Lutheran-Roman Catholic and Anglican-Roman Catholic bilateral conversations. A parallel dialogue between Anglicans and Lutherans, it was hoped, would both benefit from and contribute to the other two bilateral discussions. This commission met four times between September 1970 and April 1972 when it approved its report, widely spoken of as the *Pullach Report,* from the German town where the dialogue group met for its last meeting.

A joint working group was established to monitor reactions to the report. This group held an evaluation meeting in Geneva from 15 to 19 December 1975. Although the *Pullach Report* had not actually been sent on to the churches for their comment until mid-1973, a number of responses had been received when the group met. One significant comment came from the churches in Australia. The Australians suggested that there was a need to explore more fully the nature of *episcope* ("oversight"). Both Lutherans and Anglicans acknowledge the need for *episcope* in the ordering of the church. The Australians asked whether there was a shared understanding of the nature of *episcope* and whether it might be possible to acknowledge this mutually while recognizing that *episcope* might be exercised by Anglicans and Lutherans in different forms. Ultimately this suggestion would give rise to the 1987 consultation on *episcope* held at Niagara Falls.

The Joint Working Group recommended the establishment of a bilateral commission for the European region which would deal with questions of ministry and eucharist as well as consider the work of the Faith and Order Commission on baptism, eucharist, and ministry. The bilateral commission in the United States, established in 1969, was given responsibility for discussing the topic, "What is the Gospel?" Because the numbers of Anglicans and Lutherans in Tanzania were roughly equal and the two churches were on friendly terms, the Tanzanian churches were given the responsibility to work toward the realization of some form of joint local mission, e.g., theological education, social welfare, urban/rural mission. Finally, the Geneva meeting recommended that the Joint Working Group meet again in about three years' time to review further progress.

Nothing, of course, ever goes absolutely as planned. The World Council of Churches' document, *Baptism, Eucharist and Ministry,* would take longer to develop than the Joint Working Group anticipated and it did not appear until 1982. Consequently, the European Commission did not publish its report, *Anglican-Lutheran Dialogue: The Report of the European Commission*, until 1983. In that report the commission concluded that, on the basis of the agreement already reached between the two churches, there were no serious obstacles to the establishment of full communion between the two churches (paragraph 62).

The American dialogue did not publish their study on the gospel until 1978. As a result, the Joint Working Group did not meet again until 1983, by which time considerable progress had occurred in the American dialogue. However, before passing on to the American dialogue and the shift to the quest for full communion, something needs to be said about the dialogue between the Church of England and the Evangelical Church in Germany (EKD) and the so-called *Meissen Agreement: On the Way to Visible Unity.*

The *Meissen Agreement*, which came into effect in 1991, is of particular interest because it is a first step toward visible unity between episcopal and non-episcopal churches. The agreement has a limited recognition of ministries. Anglican priests, for example, are eligible for pastoral appointments in the EKD, but, because of English statute law, German pastors are not eligible to hold benefices in the Church of England. The agreement explicitly excludes participation in the laying on of hands at each other's ordinations.

The churches of the *Meissen Agreement* mutually recognize one another as belonging to the one apostolic Church and as participating in the common apostolic mission. The churches officially encourage their members to worship with and receive communion in the partner church. The churches commit themselves to common life and mission as geography permits. An implementation commission exists to monitor the agreement and to iron out any difficulties that might arise.

(b) The Quest for Full Communion

The basic issues between Anglicans and Lutherans with regard to ordained ministry focus on whether there is one order of ordained ministry or three and on the significance of the historic episcopate. Lutherans are confessionally committed to recognizing an ordered ministry as a gift of God to the Church, but the same confessions commit Lutherans to no specific structure of ordered ministry. Anglicans, on the other hand, while not identifying the historic episcopate with the very existence of the church, are committed to maintaining the historic threefold ministry and can foresee no possibility of a united church apart from the historic episcopate. Nevertheless, there is considerable common ground between the two traditions on ordained ministry, not the least of which includes the insight that apostolicity is not reducible to a tactile succession of ordained ministers and that the apostolic succession of the ministry functions within the apostolic succession of the Church as a whole. Since both traditions acknowledge the need for an extra-parochial office of oversight, it was hoped that an international consultation on *episcope* might provide an opportunity for seeing a way forward.

This meeting took place in Niagara Falls, Ontario, in late September of 1987. Its outcome was *The Niagara Report: Report of the Anglican-Lutheran Consultation on Episcope 1987*, which appeared in 1988 in time for consideration by the Lambeth Conference of that year. The report focuses on *episcope* in the context of the mission of the Church. The reasoning behind that decision was simply that the Church does not exist for itself; it exists for a purpose. That purpose sets the Church apart from other institutions and that purpose shapes the instrumentalities of the Church.

The wider ecumenical climate against which *The Niagara Report* developed includes an emphasis on *koinonia* ("communion") as fundamental for an understanding of the Church. Indeed, the Church may be defined as the *communion of believers with God, Father, Son, and Holy Spirit, and with each other.* Such a definition roots the Church not only in the sending of the disciples by Christ, but also in the sending by the Father of the Son in the Holy Spirit. Such a definition roots the Church in that which is common to Father, Son, and Holy Spirit, namely, the eternal life that is God's own life. This rootage of our understanding of the Church is important because it allows for degrees of communion; it does not restrict us to an all or nothing situation.

Such an emphasis on *Trinitarian communion* is more implicit than explicit in *The Niagara Report* which begins with our reception of God's gifts poured out in Christ (paragraph 11). It does, however, give explicit expression to this reality when it notes that apostolicity means "that the Church is sent by Jesus to *be* for the world, to participate in his mission and therefore in the mission of the One who sent Jesus, to participate in the mission of the Father and the Son through the dynamic of the Holy Spirit" (paragraph 21). The report then goes on to identify six requirements for the Church's mission: (i) doxology, (ii) continuity, (iii) disciplined life together, (iv) nurture, (v) direction and goal, and (vi) development of structure (paragraphs 27–59).

The mere presence of a bishop will not guarantee the continuity of apostolic faith just as the mere absence of a bishop does not by itself guarantee loss of continuity in apostolic faith. But within the graced human response to God's continuing activity, the continuity of ordained ministry is a powerful symbol of continuity in faith. Indeed, it is so powerful a symbol that where that continuity is found there is a presumption of continuity in faith and where that continuity is breached there is a presumption of a breach in the continuity of faith. Both Anglicans and Lutherans face the same problem in the wider ecumenical scene. The succession in the presiding ministry of their respective churches no longer incontestably links those churches to the *koinonia* of the wider Church (see paragraphs 54–58).

Anglicans are vulnerable on two grounds. First, the consecration of Matthew Parker as archbishop of Canterbury in 1559 was accomplished in an uncanonical fashion in that no currently sitting diocesan bishops could be found who were willing to consecrate him. Second, Roman Catholics argue that the liturgical changes embodied in the ordinals of 1550 and 1552 point to a doctrinal change in the understanding of ordained ministry and, consequently, are incapable of transmitting the traditional offices of bishop, presbyter, and deacon.

The Lutheran Reformation faced the refusal of sitting bishops to ordain Evangelical pastors. Initially this was not a problem as the ranks of Evangelical pastors were constituted by already episcopally ordained clergy passing into the Evangelical movement. But as time passed this migration ceased and the question of ordination became critical. In this emergency situation new pastors were ordained by persons who had already been ordained presbyters in the medieval church. Relying on the emergency nature of their situation and on St. Jerome's position on the original unity of the office of bishop and presbyter, the Evangelical movement ordained new pastors and located the authority of a bishop's office in the pastorate. The succession of presiding ministry was maintained in an unaccustomed form. Both Lutherans and Anglicans have maintained the function of *episcope*. In light of the symbolic position of those who exercise the office of *episcope* in both our communions — a position which reflects both the local and universal *koinonia* — the continued isolation of one from another of those who exercise this office of *episcope* is no longer tolerable and must be overcome, provided commonly held apostolic faith undergirds both traditions. It is precisely this commonality of apostolic faith which the report, in paragraphs 60–80, asserts is present in both traditions.

This understanding of the Church as *koinonia* has helped both traditions to understand that "full communion" means more than eucharistic fellowship, that it involves a community of life, an exchange and commitment to one another in respect of major decisions on questions of faith, order, and morals in addition to altar and pulpit fellowship. As a consequence, questions have been raised as to whether there is, in fact, any real distinction between "full communion" and "organic unity." Nevertheless, the 1988 Lambeth Conference endorsed the perception that unity must come by stages.

In order to facilitate the transition from limited communion to full communion, paragraphs 89–96 of *The Niagara Report* made four requests of Lutherans and three of Anglicans. Lutherans were asked (a) to standardize terminology so that all who exercise an ordained ministry of *episcope* are called "bishop"; (b) to elect bishops to the same tenure of office as other pastors; (c) to revise rites for the installation of bishops to include the laying on of hands by at least three bishops; and (d) to restrict the presidency of ordinations to bishops. Anglicans were asked (a) to make the necessary canonical changes to acknowledge and recognize the full authenticity of the existing ministries of the Lutheran church; (b) to establish and welcome structures for the collegial and periodic review of the bishop's ministry for the purpose of evaluating and improving the same; and (c) to invite Lutheran bishops regularly to participate in the laying on of hands in Anglican episcopal ordinations.

Since the publication of *The Niagara Report* three regional dialogues have explored the possibility of full communion between Anglicans and Lutherans. The dialogue between the Nordic/Baltic Lutheran churches and the Anglican churches of Great Britain and Ireland has been successfully concluded and full communion initiated. The American dialogue is currently preparing a revision of the concordat put to both churches in the summer of 1997 after the failure of the Evangelical Lutheran Church in America to secure the necessary two-thirds majority to approve the concordat.[2] The Canadian dialogue is still on the journey with a decision date of July 2001. A brief review of the first two of these regional dialogues is in order here.

The concordat as proposed in 1997 acknowledged an agreement in the essentials of the one, catholic, and apostolic faith as witnessed to in the *Augsburg Confession*, the *Small Catechism*, and the *Book of Common Prayer* (1979), including the "Episcopal Services" and "Outline of the Faith," and summarized in *Implications of the Gospel*, and the report which accompanies the concordat entitled *Toward Full Communion between the Episcopal Church and the Evangelical Lutheran Church in America* (published in 1991). Each church undertook to require its ordination candidates to study the basic documents of the other church. In the consecration of bishops there was to be on an invariable basis the participation of at least three bishops of each church in the laying on of hands. There was agreement between the two churches that the future pattern of the ordained ministry of Word and Sacrament in each church will be that of the threefold ministry of bishop, presbyter, and deacon.

The Episcopal Church proposed to acknowledge Lutheran pastors as priests within the Lutheran church and Lutheran bishops to be bishops within that church exercising episcopal ministry within the jurisdictions entrusted to them. Further, the Episcopal Church would

---

2 Although the General Convention of the Episcopal Church in the United States approved the concordat, the National Convention of the Evangelical Lutheran Church in America fell six votes short (690 in favour required, 684 received).

suspend the restriction limiting the exercise of ordained ministry within the Episcopal Church to those ordained by bishops in the historic succession. This suspension would permit full interchangeability and reciprocity of ordained ministries between the two churches. Finally, the concordat would have the Episcopal Church endorse the Lutheran principle that the historic episcopate is under the word of God and in the service of the gospel, thus leading to the establishment of structures for the periodic and collegial review of episcopal ministry.

On the Lutheran side the concordat would have led to ordination of Lutheran bishops for the life service of the gospel while limiting tenure in office to retirement, resignation, or other constitutionally mandated conclusion. In addition, bishops would ordain all clergy, although presbyters would continue to participate in the laying on of hands on those ordained to the presbyterate. Both churches were to recognize the diaconate and would work together in continued study and reform of the office. Finally, Episcopal bishops, presbyters, and deacons would have full interchangeability and reciprocity with their counterparts in the Lutheran church without any requirement of supplementary oaths or subscriptions.

Both churches would have established a joint commission to moderate the ecumenical, doctrinal, and liturgical dimensions of these changes and to prepare for the celebration of the inauguration of the concordat. Each church would remain in full communion with those churches with which it was already in communion and neither church would be automatically included in these pre-existing arrangements. Both churches would establish organs of regular consultation and communication.

The second bilateral dialogue focusing on full communion is that between the British and Irish Anglican churches and the Nordic and Baltic Lutheran churches and, in a sense, brings us back to where these considerations on Anglican-Lutheran relations in the twentieth century began. From as early as 1929, with the exception of the war years, the Church of England and the Scandinavian Lutheran churches sponsored bi-annual theological conferences. Then, in 1978, a pastoral conference was organized for those years the theological conference did not meet. The new climate of theological debate created at the world level by the bilateral and multilateral dialogues during the

1970s and the 1980s, capped by the drafting of the *Meissen Statement* in 1988, was another positive contextual factor, as were two major political events: (1) the collapse of the Soviet empire leading to representatives from the Baltic churches attending the theological conference beginning in 1989, and (2) the creation of the European Union. Also, the personal initiatives of Archbishop Robert Runcie of Canterbury and Archbishop Bertil Werkström of Uppsala were not negligible elements in focusing the theological discussions. Four plenary sessions of theological conversations were held in the period from 1989 to 1992. At the last meeting in Järvenpää, Finland, the final text of a common statement was agreed to. Called *The Porvoo Common Statement*, after the cathedral city of the diocese in which Järvenpää is located, the document was published, together with a series of essays on church and ministry in northern Europe, under the title *Together in Mission and Ministry*.

The Porvoo Common Statement articulates a rationale for realizing fellowship that was not confined to the chief officeholders of the churches concerned. This task was made more difficult because each of those churches primarily exists in a country where the other churches are virtually absent. Though all of the churches are episcopally structured, three different ecclesial attitudes toward the historic episcopate were represented. Some of the churches regard the historic episcopate as a theological imperative; some of the churches have safeguarded the historical succession without seeing it as something which of necessity belongs to the nature of the church; and some of the churches, while experiencing a formal break in episcopal continuity at the time of the Reformation, have maintained a continuity in doctrine, place, and office of those exercising ministries of *episcope*.

Since the apostolicity of the ordained ministry is within the apostolic succession of the Church as a whole and since the episcopal succession is *a* sign and not *the* sign of apostolicity, a church which has preserved ". . . the sign of historical episcopal succession . . . is free to acknowledge an authentic episcopal ministry in a church which has preserved continuity in the episcopal office by an occasional priestly/presbyteral ordination at the time of the Reformation."[3]

---

3 Ibid., paragraph 52.

At this point the statement explicitly affirms the theological priority of the acknowledgment of each other's status as church and of each other's ordained ministry over any common participation in the laying on of hands in ordinations. Precisely because of this, any such participation cannot be construed as casting doubt on prior ordinations. Mutual participation in the laying on of hands in ordinations "is . . . a means of making more visible the unity and continuity of the Church at all times and in all places."[4]

---

4 Ibid., paragraph 53.

FULL COMMUNION:
Where does this phrase come from, and what does it mean?

Alyson Barnett-Cowan

Koinonia, "communion," "inter-communion," "full communion," "organic union," "real but imperfect communion," *communio in sacris*: a litany of interrelated terms is chanted throughout the ecumenical world. And throughout the ecumenical movement, there has been confusion about terminology. What one family of churches means by a term is not always the same as what another family means. That is why so much attention has been paid in bilateral and multilateral dialogues to coming to understand precisely how words and phrases are understood by all parties, and to giving a common definition, so that all parties are reading agreed statements in the same way.

Nowhere does there seem to be more confusion than when the churches try to describe precisely what the goal of full visible unity would look like if it were attained. The differing views are themselves rooted in the different self-understandings of the churches. Some envisage one unified structure; others speak of relationships of families of churches (communion of communions); others prefer a loose association of autonomous churches. The same kinds of debates which take place about the nature of a future worldwide ecumenical church also take place within our church families. Lutherans and Anglicans alike struggle with what it means to be in "communion" at the world level, and what sort of relationship ought to exist among or even over local churches.

Anglicans use the term "Communion" of themselves. The Anglican Communion is made up of local churches (provinces and, in some cases, dioceses) which are in communion with the see of Canterbury. That is the only criterion for belonging, although there are several structures ("instruments of unity") which bring Anglicans together for consultation. In addition, there is a growing number of churches which are not Anglican in origin, yet which have entered into relationships of communion with Canterbury. The 1931 *Bonn Agreement with Old Catholic Churches* established a relationship which in 1931 was termed "inter-communion," but which was renamed "full communion" in 1958. In 1965 a concordat of full communion was established with the Spanish Reformed Episcopal Church, the Lusitanian Church, and the Philippine Independent Church. Various provinces have entered concordat relationships of full communion with the Mar Thoma Syrian Church.

A new ecumenical wrinkle (while welcome!) has emerged with the entry of the Anglican provinces in England, Ireland, Scotland, and Wales into communion with the Nordic Baltic Lutheran churches. Calling themselves "the Porvoo Communion," these churches are in communion with the archbishop of Canterbury by virtue of his being head of the Church in England, and so some Lutheran bishops from the Porvoo churches were invited to the 1998 Lambeth Conference as bishops in communion. There have not yet been, however, agreements of mutual recognition with other Anglican provinces, and so the exact nature of the relationship is unclear.

The Lutheran World Federation also uses the terminology of "communion," although its preferred language is that of "confession." The constitution of the LWF (1990) defines that body as "a communion of churches which confess the Triune God, agree in the proclamation of the word of God and are united in pulpit and altar fellowship".[1]

CLAD I and II spent considerable time defining the goal of the relationship between the Evangelical Lutheran Church in Canada and the Anglican Church of Canada. As both churches are in turn members of wider international families of churches, and as both families see themselves as only part of the Body of Christ, we are aware that

---

1 *Dictionary of the Ecumenical Movement*, s.v. "Communion" (Geneva: WCC Publications, 1991).

our relationship will only be one small step along the way to the vision we all share and seek: the full visible unity of all the whole Church on earth. Yet our relationship is already more than one of mutual respect and intercommunion.

The work of the Joint Working Group has been based on an understanding of "unity by stages," which sees "full communion" as the third stage of a movement toward full visible unity. This concept has been well-articulated in the ecumenical world, and its origin is attributed to the Roman Catholic-Lutheran Joint Commission agreed statement *Facing Unity* (1984).[2] The steps are generally recognized as (1) mutual recognition of each other as churches in which the gospel is preached and taught; (2) reciprocal inter-communion (usually with non-episcopal churches); (3) full communion; and (4) organic union. Stage one was achieved by CLAD through a detailed discussion of doctrinal issues to determine that we believe and proclaim the same apostolic faith. Stage two was established as an official mutual recognition and invitation to "interim eucharistic sharing." Stage four would be a structural union, the establishment of a united church with one set of structures and one episcopacy; the Joint Working Group believes that this is premature as a proximate goal for Anglicans and Lutherans in Canada.

CLAD II recommended the following definition of "full communion," seeing it as the appropriate next step, or stage three, on the way, and it has been endorsed by both churches:

> Full communion is understood as a relationship between two distinct churches or communions in which each maintains its own autonomy while recognizing the catholicity and apostolicity of the other, and believing the other to hold the essentials of the Christian faith. In such a relationship communicant members of each church would be able freely to communicate at the altar of the other and there would be freedom of ordained

---

2 *Facing Unity: Models, Forms and Phrases of Catholic-Lutheran Fellowship* (Geneva: Lutheran World Federation, 1985).

ministers to officiate sacramentally in either church. Specifically in our context we want this to include transferability of members; mutual recognition and interchangeability of ministries; freedom to use each other's liturgies; freedom to participate in each other's ordinations and installations of clergy, including bishops; and structures for consultation to express, strengthen and enable our common life, witness and service, to the glory of God and the salvation of the world.[3]

The understanding of "full communion" is akin to the term with which Lutherans are more familiar: "pulpit and altar fellowship." In the Anglican tradition, the term "full communion" has been recommended for use in this kind of situation by the Lambeth Conference of 1958:

Resolution 14: The Conference endorses the paragraph in the Report of the Committee on Church Unity and the Church Universal which refers to the use of the terms "full communion" and "intercommunion," and recommends accordingly that where between two Churches not of the same denominational or confessional family, there is unrestricted communio in sacris, including mutual recognition and acceptance of ministries, the appropriate term to use is "full communion," and that where varying degrees of relation other than "full communion" are established by agreement between two such Churches the appropriate term is "intercommunion."

The paragraph of the report which is cited reads (underlining added):

The Committee has examined the use of the terms "full communion" and "intercommunion" in official documents in recent years. Although since 1931 the terminology used to

---

3 Paragraph 7 of "The Waterloo Declaration," in *Called to Full Communion* (Toronto: Anglican Book Centre, 1998), 9.

describe various degrees of inter-Church relationship has been inconsistent and confusing, the most common usage has been that advocated by the Lund Faith and Order Conference in 1952, whereby the term "full communion" has been kept to describe the close relation which exists between Churches of the same denominational or confessional family, such as the Churches of the Anglican Communion, and of the Orthodox, Lutheran, or Reformed "families" of Churches; whereas the term "Intercommunion" has been used to describe varying degrees of relation between Churches of one communion with a Church or Churches of another. Thus, for example, various Provinces and Churches of the Anglican Communion enjoy unrestricted *communio in sacris* with the Old Catholic Churches. Such unrestricted *communio in sacris*, involving complete sacramental fellowship and the mutual recognition and acceptance of ministries, has been described as "full intercommunion." It has however been pointed out that, although there may be a logical satisfaction in distinguishing between the "full communion"which exists between Churches which have grown up within the same family, and the "full intercommunion" which has been established with Churches outside the family, there is no distinction so far as spiritual reality is concerned. In each case there is unrestricted *communio in sacris*.

The committee therefore has concluded that it would be less confusing and indeed more true to reality to use the term "full communion" in all cases where a Province of the Anglican Communion by agreement enters into a relation of unrestricted *communio in sacris*, including the mutual recognition of ministries, with a Church outside our Communion. This would mean, for example, that the relation already existing between Churches of our Communion with the Old Catholic Churches would henceforth be described as that of "full communion," rather than "full intercommunion." The term "intercommunion" could then be used to describe the varying degrees of relation other than full communion, which already

exist, or may be established in the future, between Churches of
the Anglican family with others outside this family.[4]

Reception of this understanding took place over several years. Suc-
cessive Anglican reflection noted that there needed to be some form
of mutual consultation, a shared if limited jurisdiction, if full communion was to be more than participation in each other's worship. In
1981 the Anglican Consultative Council meeting in Newcastle upon
Tyne observed:

> Communion must be understood as involving more than li-
> turgical celebration: it surely implies a visible sharing to-
> gether in the common life of the Body of Christ. This seems
> to require some appropriate form of embodiment ... the time
> is ripe for the consideration of some regional form of fellow-
> ship which would bring appropriate (episcopal) Churches to-
> gether in common counsel and exchange.[5]

The definition given by CLAD II is based on two chief sources: the
World Council of Churches Third Assembly in New Delhi in 1961,
and the *Cold Ash Report* of 1983.

In its first statement on the unity of the church, the WCC said:

> We believe that the unity which is both God's will and his gift
> to his Church is being made visible as all in each place who
> are baptized into Jesus Christ and confess him as Lord and
> Saviour are brought by the Holy Spirit into one fully com-
> mitted fellowship, holding the one apostolic faith, preaching
> the one Gospel, breaking the one bread, joining in common
> prayer, and having a corporate life reaching out in witness
> and service to all and who at the same time are united with

---

4 J. Robert Wright, ed., *A Communion of Communions: One Eucharistic Fellowship* (New York: Seabury, 1979), 264–266.
5 ACC–5 (1981), 46.

the whole Christian fellowship in all places and all ages in such wise that ministry and members are accepted by all, and that all can act and speak together as occasion requires for the tasks to which God calls his people.[6]

CLAD II at its final meeting in Waterloo, June 1994, made explicit reference to the New Delhi statement as it formulated its statement on full communion. It is an interesting piece of ecumenical trivia that it was the Roman Catholic observer on the dialogue, Dr. Harry McSorley, who made this significant contribution to the Anglican-Lutheran project. New Delhi provides the backdrop for the particular scene which Canadian Lutherans and Anglicans are enacting in the ongoing ecumenical drama.

The 1983 meeting in England brought together an Anglican-Lutheran Working Group appointed by the Anglican Consultative Council and the Lutheran World Federation. Its *Cold Ash Report* (named for the Berkshire town in which it met) described full communion:

By full communion we here understand a relationship between two distinct Churches or communions. Each maintains its own autonomy and recognises the catholicity of the other, and each believes the other to hold the essentials of the Christian faith:

a) subject to such safeguards as ecclesial discipline may properly require, members of one body may receive the sacraments of the other;

b) subject to local invitation, bishops of one Church may take part in the consecration of the bishops of the other, thus acknowledging the duty of mutual care and concern;

---

6 W.A. Visser 't Hooft, ed., *The New Delhi Report: The Third Assembly of the World Council of Churches, 1961* (London: SCM, 1962), 116.

c) subject to Church regulation, a bishop, pastor/priest or deacon of one ecclesial body may exercise liturgical functions in a congregation of the other body if invited to do so and also, when requested, pastoral care of the other's members;

d) it is also a necessary addition and complement that there should be recognised organs or regular consultation and communication, including episcopal collegiality, to express and strengthen the fellowship and enable common witness, life and services.

To be in full communion means that Churches become interdependent while remaining autonomous. One is not elevated to be the judge of the other, nor can it remain insensitive to the other; neither is each body committed to every secondary feature of the tradition of the other. Thus the corporate strength of the Churches is enhanced in love, and an isolated independence restrained.

Full communion carries implications which go beyond sharing the same eucharist. The eucharist is a common meal, and to share in it together has implications for a sharing of life and of common concerns for the mission of the Church. To be in full communion implies a community of life, an exchange and a commitment to one another in respect of major decisions on questions of faith, order, and morals. It implies, where Churches are in the same geographical area, common worship, study, witness, evangelism, and promotion of justice, peace and love. It may lead to a uniting of ecclesial bodies if they are, or come to be, immediately adjacent in the same geographical areas. This should not imply the suppressing of ethnic, cultural or ecclesial characteristics or traditions within one communion.[7]

---

7 *Cold Ash Report*, paragraphs 25–27; cited in *The Emmaus Report*, 82–83.

The working definition which our two churches in Canada have established is not universally accepted. We are making a distinction between "full communion" and "full visible unity." Some confusion arises on the international ecumenical scene because the distinctions which are drawn here between "full communion" and "full visible unity" are not made by other churches. For the Roman Catholic Church, for example, full communion is only possible when there is agreement about authority and jurisdiction, when others are "in full communion" with the bishop of Rome, and therefore with his universal ministry of oversight.

Thus, for example, the World Council of Churches' statement adopted at Canberra, 1991 (*The Unity of the Church as Koinonia: Gift and Calling*) equates the full unity to which all the churches are called with "full communion":

> 2.1 The unity of the church to which we are called is a koinonia given and expressed in the common confession of the apostolic faith; a common sacramental life entered by the one baptism and celebrated together in one eucharistic fellowship; a common life in which members and ministries are mutually recognized and reconciled; and a common mission witnessing to the gospel of God's grace to all people and serving the whole of creation. The goal of the search for full communion is realized when all the churches are able to recognize in one another the holy, catholic and apostolic church in its fullness. This full communion will be expressed on the local and the universal levels through conciliar forms of life and action. In such communion churches are bound in all aspects of their life together at all levels in confessing the one faith and engaging in worship and witness, deliberation and action.[8]

---

8 Gunther Gassmann, ed. *Documentary History of Faith and Order, 1963–1993*, Faith and Order Paper 159 (Geneva: WCC Publications, 1993).

While the Canadian Anglican proposal would see many of these aspects of what we would call "full visible unity" realized in *The Waterloo Declaration*, it stops short of such a complete structural and jurisdictional unity, believing that the experience of lived communion by two churches which retain their own identity and decision-making structures will lead us toward that more complete goal. It does, however, call for structures for consultation. We will, if the declaration is accepted by both churches, increasingly participate in each other's decision-making bodies, so that we can grow closer together in the day to day lives of the churches, and take counsel together for our common mission. There will be areas of shared jurisdiction, particularly in shared ministry parishes, which will have an opportunity to model shared *episcope*. Already the bishops of the two churches meet together every year, and have the lived experience of collegiality.

The term which we translate "communion" is of course the Greek word, *koinonia*, which refers at its heart not to church bodies, but to the communion of persons: the perfect communion which the three Persons of the divine Trinity have with each other, and the communion with them into which human beings are invited as members of the Body of Christ. As a term for Church, it refers to a relationship of the baptized with their bishop, and through the bishop with other bishops and other faithful people in communion with those bishops. It is a web of relationships, sustained by mutual bonds of affection and common faith, nourished above all by the divine life which breathes into and transforms all our ways together. In the proposed relationship between the Anglican Church of Canada and the Evangelical Lutheran Church in Canada, the growth together in grace in the power of the Holy Spirit, the journey together in faith, life, and witness, is the truly important part of the story. We dare to hope that our being on the way together toward the common goal of unity in Christ will be blessed by the holy God who is relationship and love, and will be a small sign of the continual inbreaking of the gracious realm of God.

LUTHERAN VIEWS OF THE HISTORIC EPISCOPATE

Richard Stetson

The historic episcopate has a varied history in the Lutheran churches. Episcopal succession was consciously preserved in some and lost in others during the crisis precipitated by the sixteenth-century Reformation in Europe. In the twentieth century attitudes among Lutherans still vary.

A major international Anglican-Lutheran consultation, "Episcopé in Relation to the Mission of the Church," was held in Niagara Falls, Ontario, in 1987. Bishop Sebastian Kolowa of the Evangelical Lutheran Church in Tanzania reported that even though the ELCT had been formed in 1961 with three dioceses headed by bishops (Bukoba, Moshi, and Usambara-Digo) and three synods headed by presidents (Southern, Eastern, and Central), by 1985 most of the units of the ELCT had in principle accepted episcopacy. On the other hand, other African churches, like the Evangelical Lutheran Church in Cameroon, formed about the same time, were founded and remain non-episcopal.

A missionary with many years of experience in southern Africa observed that though some of the Lutheran churches there started with bishops ordained within the historic succession and some did not, it is now impossible to say which churches have succession and which do not. At the celebration of any new episcopal ministry, neighbouring bishops join enthusiastically in the laying on of hands and prayer, whether or not they are in historic succession. Thus the succession has spread out of the pure joy of fellowship and spirit of collegiality among the bishops and churches rather than through any conscious agreement or design.

This is quite different from the attitude of some other Lutherans in regard to this issue. A Church of Sweden priest once related the story of attending an ordination in the Church of Denmark. The Danish bishop instructed the Swedish priest to stay at least three metres away from the ordinands at all times during the liturgy, so that there would be no possibility of thinking that any of the candidates had been ordained into the succession of the Swedish Lutheran Church.

As Lutherans see no particular polity as commanded by God or instituted in scripture, there are Lutheran churches with bishops in the historic succession and others that are episcopal but lack historic succession. There are churches that are governed synodically and some that are quite congregationalist. If formal intercommunion does not exist between Lutheran church bodies, it is due to perceived doctrinal differences, not issues of polity. And, all member churches of the Lutheran World Federation are in communion with one another, regardless of polity.

At times the sixteenth-century Lutheran confessional documents do speak on the office of bishop. Article 28 of the *Augsburg Confession* of 1530 says that the bishop "according to divine right" is to preach the gospel, administer the sacraments, forgive sins, condemn teaching that is contrary to the gospel, and exclude from the community of Christ any whose conduct is a public scandal. The congregations and parish ministers are bound to obedience to the bishop by the word of Christ, "He who hears you, hears me" (Luke 10:16). But if bishops introduce anything contrary to the gospel, Christians have God's command not to obey them (Matthew 7:15, Galatians 1:8, 2 Corinthians 13:8).

The *Apology* (defence) *of the Augsburg Confession* clearly affirms the willingness of the Lutheran reformers "to keep the ecclesiastical and canonical polity, provided the bishops stop raging against our churches. This willingness will be our defense, both before God and among all nations, present and future, against the charge that we have undermined the authority of bishops."

Episcopacy is never rejected in principle, but as the Lutheran confessional documents of the sixteenth century speak on the office of bishop, the chief concern is the confusion of the power of bishops with "the temporal sword." It is expected that the office will be retained but in a purified form stripped of the secular powers and prestige accumulated by many medieval bishops.

The episcopate is to be retained and respected for the sake of love and unity in the Church. Once again, the historic episcopate was not lost in any Lutheran church because it was rejected in principle, but because the reformers objected where the bishop refused to ordain candidates for the priesthood considered suitable by the reforming parishes. The German version of the *Apology of the Augsburg Confession*, Article 28, complains bluntly that the bishops "ordain crude asses."

In 1545, Elector John Fredrick, ruler of Saxony, requested a formal opinion (*Ratschlag*) of the theologians of Wittenberg on the role of a reformed bishop. The theologians answered unequivocally that the bishop's role is "to keep order in the church." The theologians called for bishops, "a degree higher than priests, with designated authority." They also asked for synods, chaired by the bishop, to work out problems, promote unity and care for the universities, serving as "custodians of doctrine." Examples like Athanasius, Ambrose, and Augustine were cited as bishops who corrected false teaching and fought heresy. Their conclusion is direct: "If the existing form of episcopacy were torn apart (*zerrissen*), barbarism and desolation without end would result, for temporal power and princes are burdened with other matters, and only a few respect the church or reflect on its teaching."[1]

Evangelical episcopates were established in some German cities for a time. There were Lutheran bishops in Naumberg (1542–1551), Schleswig-Holstein (1542–1551), Merseburg (1544–1550), and Kammin (1545–1556).[2] Martin Luther himself participated in the first ordinations of evangelical bishops in Naumberg and Merseburg. Other forms of polity also emerged, consistories or synods with oversight exercised by superintendents, provosts, or deans appointed by the local prince acting as "emergency bishop" (*Notsbischöfe*).

This situation developed from a statement by Luther in the wake of the crisis following a noted debate at Leipzig in 1519 between Luther and the Dominican John Eck. Luther lost that debate, according to

---

1 Eric W. Gritsch, "From Servanthood to Serpenthood: Decision-Making in the Church," *Dialog* 37 (Summer 1998), 213.
2 Ibid., 213.

the umpires from the Universities of Paris and Erfurt, for asserting that councils of the church could err. Having lost faith in the ability of ecclesiastical councils to reform the church, Luther turned to another "council" that of the "Christian nobility of the German nation." In a polemical appeal in 1520 Luther advocated the destruction of "three walls" of the church that represented abuse of power. Luther attacked any notion that God had instituted a difference between clergy and laity, that the pope is the sole interpreter of scripture, and the assertion that the pope alone could call an ecumenical council. His most radical proposal was that the German princes, as baptized noblemen, should take leadership as the church's "emergency bishops."[3]

Luther died in 1546, never seeing the final development of this proposal. The *Peace of Augsburg* of 1555 dictated that the ruler of a particular region has the power to decide its religion. This was soon interpreted in Lutheran areas that the princes who had previously functioned only as "emergency bishops" would assume full authority for overseeing the church, becoming known as *summi episcopi*. This situation prevailed in Germany until the collapse of the monarchy in 1918 when democratic reform demanded different forms of church organization.

Sixteenth-century German reformers, in need of pastors for the congregations, deduced on the basis of scripture and patristic evidence in the writings of St. Jerome, that there was no difference *de iure divino* between the office of priest and bishop. Ordination had been reserved to the bishops *de iure humano*. They held that no generally accepted theology of development has emerged by which it may be explained how second- and third-century developments like episcopal structure are to be regarded as being of divine authority. Lutherans had come to the conclusion that church polity is not given by divine authority; therefore the church may adopt whatever structures serve the gospel in a given time and place.

Apostolic succession was interpreted as *successio evangelii*. Therefore any suggestion that anything could be as important as the gospel

---

3 Ibid., 212.

in unifying the Church is still treated with the utmost suspicion by many Lutherans. The *satis est* ("it is enough") clause in the seventh article of the *Augsburg Confession* is their standard.

> For the true unity of the church *it is enough* to agree concerning the teaching of the Gospel and the administration of the sacraments. It is not necessary that human traditions or rites and ceremonies, instituted by men, should be alike everywhere." (italics added)

In Sweden, where historic episcopal succession is maintained, the first Lutheran Archbishop of Uppsala, Larentius Petri, prepared a major document of the Swedish Reformation, the *Church Ordinance* of 1571. In this church ordinance the ministry of the bishop is considered a gift "without doubt emanating from God the Holy Spirit (as giver of all good gifts)." The ordinance states that the episcopate is to be continued in the church "as long as the world remains."

The Swedish bishops' understanding of episcopacy expressed to the Lambeth Conference's invitation to intercommunion early in this century shows both the solidarity and tension that is part of the dynamic of the Swedish reformation with developments on the continent. The following points are from the statement of the Swedish bishops as recorded in the Swedish *Kyrkohistorisk årsskrift* of 1923.

> 4. The object of any organization and of the whole ministry being included in the preaching of the Gospel and the administration of the sacraments — according to the fifth article of the Augustana , God has instituted "*ministerium docendi evangelii et porrigendi sacramenta*" — our Church cannot recognize any essential difference, de *jure divino*, of aim and authority between the two or three orders into which the ministry of grace may have been divided, *jure humano*, for the benefit and convenience of the Church.

> 5. The value of every organization of the ministerium ecclesiasticum, and of the Church in general, is only to be judged by its fitness and ability to become a pure vessel for the su-

pernatural contents, and a perfect channel for the way of Divine Revelation unto mankind.

6. That doctrine in no wise makes our Church indifferent to the organization and the forms of ministry which the cravings and experiences of the Christian community have produced under the guidance of the Spirit in the course of history. We do not only regard the peculiar forms and traditions of our Church with the reverence due to a venerable legacy from the past, but we realize in them a blessing from the God of history accorded to us.

Non-Lutheran churches that preserve the episcopal succession have often viewed it as the chief link in apostolic succession and if past and current ministries are deemed invalid due to the absence of episcopal succession, it still must be rejected in the Lutheran mind.

Scholars have pointed out that though Lutherans have usually emphasized faithfulness to the gospel as the sign of true apostolic succession, there is also a concern for the orderly transmission of the ministry of the Word and Sacraments. Dr. A. C. Piepkorn noted in his research for the Lutheran-Roman Catholic dialogue in the United States that even though the Lutheran Confessions do not discuss any necessity of a succession of ministry, they operate with a de facto concept of succession in that they require the churches to use their own pastors for the ordination of new clergy (*Smalcald Articles*, III, 9, and *Treatise on the Power and Primacy of the Pope*, 72). As early as the seventeenth century, a Danish Lutheran theologian, Hans Vandal, noted that there are at least three aspects of apostolic succession: succession of persons, succession of sees, and succession of apostolic doctrine.[4]

As the seventh article of the *Augsburg Confession* states, where the gospel is taught rightly and the sacraments administered faithfully there is an authentic church and ministry. Lutherans are not accustomed to reversing the process and looking at a "valid" ministerial office as proof

---

4 Toivo Harjunpaa, "Apostolic Succession and its Ecumenical Significance, Part III," *Reconcile* 3 (July 1981), 5.

of a community's faithfulness to the gospel and apostolicity. As validity is not a concept that is necessarily determined by its recognition, in the traditional terms of Latin theology, the *res* (matter) of apostolicity can be present even when the *signum* (sign or seal) of episcopal succession is not.

Even when the desirability of episcopacy as the normal structure of the church is granted, some Lutherans argue that the historic episcopate is still so absolutized by some churches that the abuses which caused it to be dispensed with in the Reformation still exist. Any suggestion that the historic episcopate is a necessary guarantee for the unity and faith of the Church is rejected on the basis of the Lutheran teaching of the primacy of the gospel.

Dr. Faith Rohrbaugh, in her background paper for *The Niagara Report*, "Episcope and the Laity," recalls some interesting historical perspectives in North America as well.[5] Early eighteenth-century Lutheran immigrants to North America often founded congregations before they had clergy. In adjusting to the new world they organized in more democratic forms than had been the custom in most of Europe. A late sixteenth-century church order developed in the Netherlands where Lutherans were a religious minority was taken as a model. This church order directed that all church leaders, including the pastor, be elected and that a two-thirds vote of the communicant members would be required in all important decisions. Synods were later formed, often with the clergy as the only voting members, as the need for overseeing the standards, education, and ordination of clergy became evident. But congregations usually still retained control of most of their own affairs and a clergy president, elected for a stated term, presided over the synod rather than a bishop. This was likely as much a product of cultural influences as any other concern, pastoral or theological. Dr. Rohrbaugh quotes Dr. Timothy Lull. Lull observed (in overly simplistic terms by his own admission) that Lutherans often begin with the concept of the congregation and ask what if anything else may be needed to express the fullness of the church. Roman

---

5 Faith E. Burgess, *Papers of the Consultation*, 130–136.

Catholics (and others) may begin with the bishop and all other manifestations of the church, including the local parish, derive their reason for being from him.

Other voices are also heard, emphasizing the importance of the sign of the historic episcopate to historic churches with whom we seek unity. It has been proposed that if episcopal succession is of great importance to partners seeking communion and the visible unity of the Church and Lutherans have no objection in principle, then a course of accommodation by Lutherans is mandated. Deferring to others in this matter does not require agreement that episcopal succession is of the same theological importance given by some churches, but it places us clearly in the camp of those who are seeking the unity for which Christ prayed and are not too proud to say that they have something to gain from other churches.

> ... the discussion of the historic episcopate among [Lutherans] will go nowhere if it throws the slightest doubt upon the authenticity of Lutheran ministry now and in centuries past. The fullness and effectiveness of the saving and sanctifying grace of God exercised through these ministries cannot be put into question. At the same time, if we say that Christian unity is a process of mutual enrichment, we dare not say that we have nothing further to receive. Our inclusion in the episcopal succession shared by other Lutherans and other communions would be a great enrichment. A greater enrichment would be the reconciliation that such an inclusion would make possible.[6]

The debate on the role and value of bishops in the church is not yet settled in the eyes of some North American Lutherans. The relationship of the bishop to both the clergy and to the laity who minister in

---

6 Richard John Neuhaus, "Getting Serious About Bishops," *Forum Letter* 11 (26 November 1982), 2.

the world is still being worked out. The examples observed in the episcopal churches, perhaps especially within Anglicanism, will have an effect on that development. The value of bishops being in historic succession will be partly influenced by what Lutherans see happening in the churches that uphold and cherish this succession. But we dare not say we have nothing to receive from others that would enrich our own unity and the unity of the whole Christian Church.

THE WATERLOO DECLARATION AND THE MINISTRY OF BISHOPS

Richard G. Leggett

Anglicans are accustomed to speaking about their bishops as successors to the apostles. In doing so they have emphasized the historic continuity of bishops from one generation to another, even when there has been a threat to this continuity as there was during the period of the Commonwealth in England in the seventeenth century. It is faithful to a basic Anglican theological conviction that spiritual realities do not exist in the abstract but are embodied in the concrete dimensions of human life.

This conviction may raise questions in the minds of some about plans for full communion that do not include the historic episcopate as a precondition for the establishment of full communion. The questions are legitimate, but it is helpful to clarify some of the basic convictions that have shaped the approach taken by *The Waterloo Declaration* to full communion between the Anglican Church of Canada and the Evangelical Lutheran Church in Canada.

1. What is the relationship of the historic episcopate to apostolicity?

From time to time Anglicans and other Christians with an episcopal polity have spoken about the apostolic quality of the episcopate as if it were a guarantee of the apostolicity of the church. In other words, no bishops, no apostolic church. This attitude, however, has not characterized ecumenical discussions in the twentieth century, especially those conversations in which Anglicans have played a part.

The first Canadian Lutheran-Anglican Dialogue described apostolicity as "continuity in the permanent characteristics of the Church of the apostles".[1] The dialogue went on to say the following.

> [Apostolicity] is God's gift in Christ through the Holy Spirit. It is not confined to the historic episcopate but is a diverse reality which expresses itself in the teaching, mission and ministry of the whole Church.[2]

This emphasis on the apostolicity of the church is central to subsequent discussions between Anglicans and Lutherans. In *The Niagara Report* we read that ". . . apostolicity means that the Church is sent by Jesus to *be* for the world, to participate in his mission and therefore in the mission of the One who sent Jesus, to participate in the mission of the Father and the Son through the dynamic of the Holy Spirit."[3] The most recent reiteration of this conviction is found in the so-called *Porvoo Declaration*.

> Apostolic tradition in the Church means continuity in the permanent characteristics of the Church of the apostles: witness to the apostolic faith, proclamation and fresh interpretation of the Gospel, celebration of baptism and the eucharist, the transmission of ministerial responsibilities, communion in prayer, love, joy and suffering, service to the sick and needy, unity among the local churches and sharing the gifts which the Lord has given to each.[4]

If apostolicity is a characteristic of the church, then what is the role of the historic episcopate? In its 1986 report CLAD described episcopal ministry as follows.

---

1 *CLAD I*, paragraph 21.
2 Ibid., paragraph 21.
3 *Niagara*, paragraph 21.
4 *Porvoo*, paragraph 36.

Within the Body of Christ the Holy Spirit confers a variety of ministries among which is a ministry of leadership bearing the authority of Christ over against the community and expressed in oversight (*episcope*) which involves fidelity to the apostolic faith, its proclamation and embodiment in church life today and its transmission to future generations. This special ministry of leadership becomes the focus and personal symbol of Apostolic Ministry.[5]

The Niagara Report in its statement of "the truths we share" states "that a ministry of pastoral oversight (*episcope*), exercised in personal, collegial and communal ways, is necessary to witness to and safeguard the unity and apostolicity of the Church."[6]   Later in the same report, the committee expresses its belief that ". . . the apostolic succession in the episcopal office does not consist primarily in an unbroken chain of those ordaining to those ordained, but in a succession in the presiding ministry of a church, which stands in the continuity of the apostolic faith."[7]

In the light of these affirmations the historic episcopate is understood not as a guarantor of the apostolicity of the church but as a significant sign.

To ordain a bishop in historic succession (that is, in intended continuity from the apostles themselves) is also a sign. In so doing the Church communicates its care for continuity in the whole of its life and mission, and reinforces its determination to manifest the permanent characteristics of the Church of the apostles.[8] ...

The use of the sign of the historic episcopal succession does not by itself guarantee the fidelity of a church to every aspect of the apostolic faith, life and mission. There have been schisms in the history of churches using the sign of historic

---

5 *CLAD I*, paragraph 26.
6 *Niagara*, paragraph 69.
7 Ibid., paragraph 94.
8 *Porvoo*, paragraph 50.

succession. Nor does the sign guarantee the personal faithfulness of the bishop. Nonetheless, the retention of the sign remains a permanent challenge to fidelity and to unity, a summons to witness to, and a commission to realize more fully, the permanent characteristics of the Church of the apostles.[9]

Such an understanding of the historic episcopate does not minimize the sign. Rather it sets this sign in the context of the overall fidelity of the church to the apostolic teaching, mission, and ministry.

> . . . Anglicans treasure the historic episcopate as part of their own history and do not foresee full integration of ministries (i.e., full communion) apart from the historic episcopate, and . . . Lutherans, while valuing the historic succession as a sign of unity and continuity, are convinced that the historic episcopate is acceptable only where it serves the Gospel and furthers the unity of the Church, and is not acceptable as a necessity for the existence of the Church or its ministry. [10] . . .

This leads us not to ask whether a church's *ministry* is apostolic, but whether we can recognize another *church* as apostolic.

> We therefore conclude that it is possible for Anglicans and Lutherans to acknowledge each other as churches where the Gospel is truly preached and taught and to acknowledge that the other possesses a ministry of Word and Sacrament that is fruitful in terms of faith and salvation for its members. We further believe that it is possible for Lutherans and Anglicans to affirm that the other possesses a ministry of Word and Sacrament which derives from the teaching of the apostles and the practice of the early Church.[11]

---

9   Ibid., paragraph 51.
10   *CLAD I*, paragraph 37(b).
11   Ibid., paragraph 32.

Notwithstanding this affirmation, there are still two more questions that Anglicans will wish to ask.

2. Is it possible to have the *substance* of episcopal ministry without the *sign* of the historic episcopate?

Within the Anglican Communion the ministry of the bishop has been a subject of discussion throughout the centuries, but in recent decades the ecumenical movement has brought a new focus to these discussions.

In the report of the first Canadian Lutheran-Anglican Dialogue episcopal ministry was described as involving "oversight, pastoral leadership and coordination."[12] A year later the Niagara consultation on *episcope* made several specific recommendations, so that episcopal ministry in the Lutheran tradition would take a shape more easily recognizable to Anglicans: (i) all ordained persons exercising *episcope* should receive the title "bishop"; (ii) all bishops should be elected to the same tenure as congregational pastors, i.e., until tenure is terminated by death, retirement, or resignation, and structures for the periodic and collegial review of bishops be put in place; (iii) rites for the installation of bishops should be revised to require the laying on of hands by at least three bishops and, if full communion exists, one of the bishops should be from the Anglican Communion; and (iv) bishops should preside at all ordinations.[13] In turn, Anglicans were asked to act on three recommendations: (i) Anglicans should enact the necessary canonical legislation to recognize the authenticity of existing Lutheran ministries; (ii) structures for the periodic and collegial review of bishops should be welcomed and established; and, (iii) Lutheran bishops

---

12 Ibid., paragraph 30.
13 *Niagara*, paragraphs 89–92.

should be invited regularly to share in the laying on of hands at the ordination of Anglican bishops.[14]

Canadian Lutherans were clear in the affirmation of the direction of the Niagara recommendations.

> The term "bishop" is already in wide use among Lutherans worldwide including the ELCIC. This is seen to be in keeping with the historic practice of the Church and indeed is acknowledged in the Lutheran Confessions . . . . The term "bishop" is, however, seen as appropriately signifying the pastoral nature of the office and is recognized as conforming to the major tradition of the church through its history. . . . Lutherans do believe there is an office of oversight in the church divinely instituted. The use of the term "bishop" to designate the one who occupies that office is biblically, confessionally and historically acceptable.[15]

Although the Lutheran members expressed some concern about the recommendation regarding tenure, they were not "unalterably opposed to the principle of unspecified tenure for bishops."[16] Further, the Lutherans indicated that the recommendation that only bishops preside at ordinations was already the present practice of the Evangelical Lutheran Church in Canada and that, when the bishop is unable to be present, the bishop authorizes an ordained representative to preside.[17]

The Canadian Anglican response to *The Niagara Report* indicated ". . . that the full Anglican tradition . . . admits to the possibility of the validity of ordinations by presbyters which attest to a long and uninterrupted practice of episcopal ordination".[18] In the concluding paragraph of the explanatory material to the *Porvoo Declaration* we read

---

14 Ibid., paragraphs 94-96.
15 CLAD II, "Lutheran Response," paragraph 2.
16 Ibid., paragraph 3.
17 Ibid., paragraph 5.
18 Ibid., "Anglican Response," paragraph 13.

". . . those churches in which the sign (of the historic episcopal succession) has been used are free to recognize the reality of the episcopal office and should affirm the apostolic continuity of those churches in which the sign of episcopal succession has at some time not been used."[19]

It is significant to note that in 1997 the National Convention of the Evangelical Lutheran Church in Canada overwhelmingly approved a resolution indicating that church's willingness to consider installation of bishops as ordination to life service of the gospel. The Council of General Synod of the Anglican Church of Canada also indicated that it was prepared to understand the ministry of the bishop in the light of Paragraph 94 of *The Niagara Report*.

We have seen that Anglican-Lutheran conversations have led to (a) an understanding of apostolicity as being vested in the church and the historic episcopate as a sign of that apostolicity and (b) a recognition of the substance of episcopal ministry in a church without the sign of the historic succession. One more question remains for us to answer.

3. Is the historic episcopate a precondition or a consequence of full communion?

Since the Lambeth Conference of 1888 Anglicans have envisioned full communion as being realizable when the partners share four fundamental signs of the apostolic church: (1) the Holy Scriptures of the Old and New Testament as containing all things necessary for salvation, (2) the Apostles' and Nicene Creeds as sufficient summaries of the faith, (3) the two dominical sacraments of baptism and eucharist,

---

19 *Porvoo*, paragraph 57.

and (4) the historic episcopate as adapted to local needs. In this construction the historic episcopate is understood as a precondition for full communion.

More recent conversations have, however, begun to ask whether the historic episcopate cannot be a consequence rather than a precondition. Within the Church of South India, for example, episcopally-ordained and presbyterally-ordained presbyters ministered together for several decades until, by natural attrition through retirement and death, all clergy in the church were episcopally-ordained. All members of that church understood this process to be undertaken for the visible unity of all of Christ's body and not a renunciation of the apostolic efficacy of the non-episcopally ordained.

The Anglican members who prepared the 1993 *Response to the Niagara Report* were quite clear in their convictions that full communion was possible without the precondition of the historic episcopate.

> To recognize each other as "sister churches" is to take a position which forbids us from living our lives apart. That living together is most graphically symbolized by an interchangeability of people and ordained ministers. To refuse this interchangeability is to adopt an attitude which is fundamentally schismatic.[20]

> If canonical change to "acknowledge and recognize the full authenticity of the existing ministries" of the Evangelical Lutheran Church in Canada by permitting clergy of that Church to serve in the Anglican Church of Canada is one such concrete expression (of our recognition of each other as "sister churches"), regularly inviting Lutheran bishops to participate in the laying on of hands at the consecration of bishops of the Anglican Church of Canada is another such expression. It graphically symbolizes the mutual involvement of those who exercise regional *episcope* in both churches in the on-going expression of that *episcope*.[21]

---

20 *CLAD II*, "Anglican Response," paragraph 14.
21 Ibid., paragraph 15.

Perhaps the most significant expression of Anglican willingness to accept the historic episcopate as a consequence rather than as a precondition is the Porvoo agreement between the British and Irish Anglican churches and the Scandinavian and Baltic Lutheran churches. In this agreement the British and Irish churches agree to enter into full communion with Lutheran churches which, while preserving the sign of bishops in historic succession, have not always preserved the episcopal ordination of bishops and presbyters.

> The mutual acknowledgement of our churches and ministries is theologically prior to the use of the sign of the laying on of hands in the historic succession. Resumption of the use of the sign does not imply an adverse judgement on the ministries of those churches which did not previously make use of the sign. It is rather a means of making more visible the unity and continuity of the Church at all times and in all places.[22]

In the joint declaration the churches involved commit themselves (a) "to welcome persons episcopally ordained in any of our churches to the office of bishop, priest or deacon to serve, by invitation and in accordance with any regulations which may from time to time be in force, in that ministry in the receiving church without re-ordination" *Porvoo*, 1993, paragraph 58(b)(v) and (b) "to invite one another's bishops normally to participate in the laying on of hands at the ordination of bishops as a sign of the unity and continuity of the Church."[23]

Having considered these three questions, let us now turn to *The Waterloo Declaration* itself.

4. The Waterloo Declaration and Episcopacy

The Waterloo Declaration is based upon several key convictions. First, apostolicity is a characteristic of the whole Church. Episcopal minis-

---

22 *Porvoo*, paragraph 53.
23 Ibid., paragraph 58(b) (vi).

try is both a sign of and a servant of apostolicity within the Church. Second, the substance of episcopal ministry may be present in a church even if the sign of the historic episcopal succession is not. Third, the resumption of the sign of the historic episcopal succession may come as a consequence of full communion rather than as a precondition for the establishment of full communion. These three convictions are based on the degree of convergence which we see in the two Canadian Lutheran-Anglican dialogues, in the Niagara consultation, and in the Porvoo process.

The provisions of *The Waterloo Declaration* respect the dignity of both churches. The existing ministries of both churches are recognized as being "fruitful in terms of faith and salvation for (the members of the two churches)" and as deriving "from the teaching of the apostles and the practice of the early Church."[23]

Neither church is asked to abandon its convictions regarding the order of the church. Whereas Anglicans are asked to accept the existing ministries of the Lutheran church, they are not asked to abandon their commitment to the historic succession of bishops as a visible sign of the church's unity and continuity. Whereas Lutherans are asked to accept the practice of episcopal ordination, they are not asked to adopt any particular understanding of the episcopate that might call to question the validity of their existing ministries.

Further, *The Waterloo Declaration* respects the context of the Canadian Anglican and Lutheran churches. Unlike the churches party to the Porvoo process, Canadian Anglican and Lutherans live side by side with overlapping jurisdictions. While the day may come when more organic unity is deemed desirable by both churches, the foreseeable future will see our two churches working side by side in mission and ministry. In this context the recognition of the authenticity of existing orders and a process by means of which the historic succession will be a consequence of our full communion seems faithful and fair.

---

24 *CLAD I*, paragraph 32.

A LUTHERAN UNDERSTANDING OF DIACONAL MINISTRY

Anne Keffer

At the outset it must be stated that I know of no clear, comprehensive, and unified Lutheran understanding of diaconal ministry. There seems to be no one statement describing diaconal ministry to which all Lutherans in Canada or North America would subscribe. When asked to write a substantive paper outlining *the* "Lutheran Understanding of Diaconal Ministry," I undertook the assignment knowing full well it cannot yet be done. What I offer here is my understanding, informed by my own experience. The two Lutheran churches whose perspective I speak from (ELCA and ELCIC, see above) both have diaconates. The question which both have addressed is whether a diaconal minister is an ordained or a lay ministry.

I will draw heavily upon two documents and some of their supporting papers. I was part of the task force on forms of ministry for the ELCIC (1986–1990) and attended the national convention in Edmonton, 1991. I am part of the Deaconess Community of the ELCA and was on the board for that community at the time when that church was considering diaconal ministry.

What I consider to be some of my formative and informative experiences are the following: hands were laid on my head by ordained pastors and deaconesses, with prayer in the assembly of God's people, in a liturgy to set me apart/consecrate me as a deaconess.[1] I received

---

1 On the wall in my office is a certificate, duly sealed by the Lutheran Church in America, which states: "Be it known that Sister Elizabeth Anne Keffer was set apart to the Office of DEACONESS according to the Confession and Constitution of the Lutheran Church In America on the 13th day of September in the year of our Lord, 1964."

theological training both within a deaconess school and in a Lutheran seminary. I received professional training in education, counselling, and spiritual direction. When entering a new ministry, I have done so as a result of having been *called* to that ministry by a congregation or by the appropriate synod council (such *call* used the same format and regulations as that used by ordained pastors).

In Two Lutheran Churches: Canada and the United States

At present in both the United States and Canada, by decision of the respective churches, diaconal ministry is a lay ministry. A task force was formed in each church as each newly merged church organized in the late 1980s and early 1990s. In each case the task force arrived at a recommendation for diaconal *ordination* which was not presented to their respective churches for approval. When the political climate had been assessed and input received, both task forces withdrew to a recommendation that would gain acceptance, hoping for a kind of "next step" approach for the future. Both reports express an interest in and a commitment to working ecumenically, especially with those groups that have permanent diaconates. The *BEM* document was part of the background information for both task forces.

The process used by both task forces was that of issuing an interim report, receiving feedback and input, then after revisions according to that feedback, making recommendation to their respective churches in convention. The ELCIC task force issued a major report in 1990, recommending a threefold form of ordained ministry. As a result of church-wide feedback and commentary, the report was revised and presented to the convention of the ELCIC in Edmonton, 1991. The written recommendation had changed to a "twofold ministry expressed in three forms: pastor, bishop, and diaconal minister."[2]

---

2 *Ministry in the Evangelical Lutheran Church in Canada: Its Forms and Practice* (March 1991).

However, at the convention itself, even that was changed, and the ELCIC convention "received" the report named *Ministry in the Evangelical Lutheran Church in Canada: Its Forms and Practice* and affirmed that "this church will have pastors, bishops and diaconal ministers."[3] Although less than originally desired, nonetheless this was a critical and important step, which few in the church have since recognized. A diaconate instituted by a church has seldom occurred. The Division for Theological Education and Leadership was instructed to study further how pastors, bishops, and diaconal ministers were to be set apart for their tasks.

In the ELCA a similar process took place a few years later. Ordination for diaconal ministers was recommended in the report, *Together for Ministry: Final Report and Recommendations, Task Force on the Study of Ministry, 1988–93.* However, the board of the Division for Ministry and the church council of the ELCA, in reviewing the report, recommended that diaconal ministry be established as a lay ministry which then became the decision of the ELCA convention, 1993.

The parallel actions and will of the people in these two churches need to be assessed as a telling part of the whole picture of the place of the diaconate in the Lutheran church today. I have few concrete facts other than personal experience to undergird the following statements, but here are my beliefs at this time. I will confine my comments to the Canadian scene.

The Canadian Scene: Some Blocks and Barriers

That there are blocks and barriers in the Canadian scene may become apparent when the following information is acknowledged. Since the original recommendation's acceptance in 1991 (that there will *be*

---

3 Division for Theological Education and Leadership, *Ministry in the ELCIC* (Evangelical Lutheran Church in Canada, December 1992).

diaconal ministers), ordination for diaconal ministry has not gained official acceptance. In 1993 the Board for the Division of Theological Education and Leadership presented a theological and functional recommendation for the ordination of diaconal ministry. In their written presentation they included often-asked questions and their answers, a world view of the Lutheran churches who do accept the threefold view of ordination (all but those in Canada and the USA) and standards for acceptance and continuance in diaconal ministry. The convention referred the whole matter back to the board with these instructions: provide a clearer definition of ordination, and include bishops; prepare guidelines on the "*certifying, commissioning, and rostering of Diaconal Ministers*" using the board's standards for acceptance as a basis. Somehow, diaconal ministers now would be certified and commissioned, not ordained! In 1997 the church in convention gave first reading to a change in the constitution: "This Church shall have a roster of lay diaconal ministers." Obviously, ordaining diaconal ministers is not something the church wishes to do at this time.

Where are these barriers and blocks coming from? How and why do they arise, even after much study, much good rationale, many good words supporting the ordination of diaconal ministry? Our church is composed of two parts, merged in 1985, which have a variety of experiences and theology. One part has had little experience and little taste for setting people apart other than clergy, professing a bias toward the congregational model of church polity. They have had little or no experience with diaconal ministry. The other, while having had the continuing services of deaconesses over a period of more than 80 years, does not hold with the theology of a threefold ordination. Thus a strong alliance against ordaining other than pastors.

At the specific request of the Division for Theological Education and Leadership prior to the 1993 convention, the two Canadian seminary faculties responded to *Ministry in the ELCIC: Its Forms and Practice* (1991). When pressed to define ordination they included not only the actual liturgy, but also the call of the community, and emphasized that such a person must be qualified. In fact, they described the whole process of education, preparation, call, liturgical recognition, and public exercise of the ministry of Word and Sacrament as ordination. They were adamant that at this time we as Lutherans do not understand ordination as a sacrament of the gospel (a means whereby the Holy Spirit communicates the gospel to persons and the church through earthly elements at the command of Christ). They held firm to the understanding of ordination as being only for those who do Word and Sacrament ministry. They also cautioned that if we are to change our understanding in the interests of ecumenism, it should be done thoroughly and slowly. While this was a report to the board and was written in the early 1990s, the faculties of our seminaries carry influence.

Yet, these are not the only forces at play, as I perceive them. I will tentatively name some others. Some have claimed there is a fear of becoming too hierarchical. But, is that understanding of hierarchy faulty? Others describe defensiveness amongst some clergy, a desire not to share power, a jealousy toward ordaining diaconal ministers. In that case, perhaps the power of ordination has been wrongly connected to position rather than to "office" and Spirit. Do we value and rightly understand the meaning of "priesthood of believers": does it prevent or preclude a wider understanding of ordination? Some say that "the way we have always done it" has become normative and thus right. "Ordination" has been studied extensively for many years in North America, but no one definition has gained ascendancy or consensus. It has been used only for pastors, and so has evolved into a cause-and-effect relationship. I have heard some of each of these perceptions, but cannot delineate the strength of their influence.

I believe there may be more. The history of the female Lutheran diaconate in Canada and the USA may be a factor in how diaconal ministry is perceived. It has always been female; it began at a time when women were not allowed to be pastors; it has been a community-based group, and as *diakonia* it is "servant." These factors may make it less appealing or less understandable in this more egalitarian and feminist period of history. Although many of us are Christian feminists and professional, well-trained women, we are often perceived as having "not quite arrived"; there is something wrong if we do not desire to be pastors.

One last factor that must be mentioned is evidenced in the action of the ELCIC in 1993: that the proposal for an ordained diaconate be "referred back to the DTEL Board for a clearer definition of ordination and the development of a proposal that includes bishops"

(National Council 93–21). How much fear surrounds the ordination of bishops? Is this, too, a power related issue? Is it based on ignorance and a prejudice for a more "congregational" polity? Whatever the cause, it is certainly a factor in this whole question. Because I stand inside the diaconate, I am sure there are other factors, which my perspective does not enable me to identify.

However, in both ELCA and ELCIC there are strong voices that challenge the church to move toward a threefold understanding of ordination. Some theologians argue that the biblical witness and the Lutheran Confessions clearly allow, if not demand, such an understanding. Others argue that for the sake of ecumenism, we must move in this direction, claiming that the Lutheran Confessions can be interpreted to accept a threefold form of ordination wholeheartedly, and that the biblical witness supports this, although it does not dictate one or another way.

Origins of Ordained Diaconal Ministry

I believe there is good authority for the ministry of *diakonia*. The ministry of Jesus Christ was a ministry of *diakonia*. "Service to persons in need was and is an essential aspect of the ministry of Jesus. Christ came not to be served but to serve. Such service is also the calling of the church and of every Christian."[4] The two task forces (ELCA and ELCIC) came to the conclusion that an ordained diaconate makes good theological and practical sense. It is interesting to note that they provide largely the same rationale. They draw from similar resources, theological arguments, and biblical texts.

> Ordaining diaconal ministers finds precedent in the history of the church. The New Testament describes a "laying on of hands" to set persons apart for a variety of ministries. From the third century there is evidence that persons were ordained

---

4 Task Force on The Study of Ministry, *Together for Ministry: Final Report and Recommendations* (Evangelical Church in America, 1994), 20.

to diaconal ministry."[5] Of utmost importance is that the service of deacons is an acting out of the Gospel, both then and now. "The office of deacon was constituted by apostolic authority through the laying on of hands to assist the apostles' proclamation of the Gospel by serving the daily needs of the community. Already in the New Testament the office of deacon became a distinct office serving together with, and under the supervision of a bishop or pastor as part of the administration of the Church. Both women and men were called into the diaconal office (Acts 6:2–6; Rom. 16:1; I Cor. 12:4–7; Phil. 1:1; I Tim. 3:10–13).[6]

The conclusions reached by both task forces are similar. "Ordained diaconal ministers will be clergy of this church who are charged with leadership of this church's diaconal mission of witness and service. Pastors and bishops will continue to exercise the ordained ministry of preaching the word and administering the sacraments."[7] "Diaconal ministers are professionally trained and ordained by the Church to serve together with a pastor or bishop. They exercise their responsibility to Word and Sacraments primarily by assisting the witness and service of the Christian community, and also by assisting in public worship."[8]

Some Historical Notes: the Lutheran "Diaconate"

The 16th century Lutheran reformers inherited a particular form of ministry from the medieval Western church....Their chief concern for ministry was ... to recover the biblical

---

5 Ibid., 13.

6 Division for Theological Education and Leadership, *Ministry in the Evangelical Lutheran Church in Canada: Its Forms and Practice* (March 1991).

7 *Together for Ministry*, 13.

8 *Ministry in the ELCIC*.

emphasis on God's ministry through the justifying ministry of Jesus Christ....They had little acquaintance with any viable form of a ministry of deacon except as a brief transition to the priesthood. In 1528 Luther himself suggested restoring a diaconate on what he took to be a New Testament or early church model. "There ought to be deacons of the church who ought to serve the bishop and to rule the church in external things according to his counsel."[9]

It wasn't until the eighteenth century that Lutheran *diakonia* was reborn. The history of modern Lutheran *diakonia* is a history of specific human need and responsive human gifts encountering each other. It began with a Lutheran pastor in Germany in 1836, and the notion spread quickly to many other European countries resulting in many institutions and thousands of women, organized under pastor-leaders. It was a product of the needs of its time. There were male deacons, but for the most part, *diakonia* became deaconesses. Pastor Theodore Fliedner, who instituted the first hospital staffed by deaconesses in Germany, regarded the office of deaconess as an ecclesiastical office, yet this whole work was instituted alongside the church. It happened. No thought-out theological foundation was provided. For women, it met the need they had for serving in a recognizable and worthwhile way as they met the many needs of the poor and the sick, the young and the old.

Women were trained in theology and in an occupation (nursing, parish work, education, social work, administration, etc.), since these two areas were considered of utmost importance. They were part of a group who supported one another in prayer. "By 1884 there were fifty-six deaconess communities (in Europe and the United States) which had a total of 5653 deaconesses."[10]

The female diaconate was transplanted to North America, to Pittsburgh, Philadelphia, Minneapolis, Chicago, Omaha, Milwaukee, and

---

9 Ibid., 7–8.
10 Frederick Weiser, *To Serve the Lord and His People* (Philadelphia, PA: Fortress Press, 1984), 11.

St. Paul in the mid- to late 1800s. In each case someone had experienced the diaconate in Europe and invited women to come from Europe to the USA where they began institutions, including a "Motherhouse" or deaconess home.

There was one notable exception. The General Synod of the Lutheran Church (USA) in 1895 created a diaconate, the first church body so to do. The Baltimore Deaconess Community and School for Parish Workers was the result of its efforts, as was the designation of deaconesses as persons holding an "office of the church." The members of this community served as parish nurses, as assistants to pastors in parishes, as teachers, at home and in the mission field. This service of deaconesses was similar to that which had developed in the Anglican, Methodist, and Presbyterian churches. The church by its action also committed itself to support and maintain this ministry.

The Office of Deaconess

The General Synod (USA) created the "office of deaconess." At that time and in that church there were two offices, one of *Word and Sacrament*, the other of deaconess. The similarities between the liturgies for ordination and for "The Setting Apart of a Deaconess" (*Occasional Services*, 1962) or "The Consecration of a Deaconess" (1918 and 1930) are evident. They both conferred an office of ministry. In the earlier edition, these words were used:

> The office of Deaconess is now committed unto you, and by the laying on of hands you are set apart for this service, In the Name of the Father, and of the Son, and of the Holy Ghost....Receive and wear this Cross, a symbol of your office of Deaconess.[11]

---

11 *The Occasional Services* (Philadelphia: The Board of Publication of The United Lutheran Church in America, 1918), 119ff.

The 1962 edition has these words:

> The chief duty of a deaconess is to assist the Ministers of the Word and the Sacraments in caring for the sick, the poor and the needy, in training the young and in reclaiming the erring and the lost. Only such as believe themselves called of God to this office can hope to understand aright its duties and only such as look to him for strength will be able to consecrate their powers to this service of Christ and his Church....The office of Deaconess is now committed unto you, and by the laying on of hands you are set apart for this service in the Church: In the Name of the Father, and of the Son and of the Holy Ghost.[12]

Did the church *intend* to have an *ordained* diaconate? They were clear that it was one of two "offices," so what else could it be? However, the word "ordination" was certainly not used. The constitution of the United Lutheran Church in America affirmed that "deaconess" was an *office of ministry* in the church and that the other such office was that of "pastor." In a subsequent church merger (1963), the description of deaconess as "office" was simply omitted from the constitution, without discussion.

As a young deaconess, I often heard the words that as deaconesses we were an office in the church. It was the treasure of being a deaconess. It meant a relationship with the whole Church, historically and professionally. It was a sacred trust from God and we were fully part of the ministry of the Church. I trained at the Baltimore School in part, and there the focus was on being the most competent professional we could be. Being part of the deaconess community was a way of enabling us to serve more effectively in those days. Because we were a community, we could afford to enable some members of the

---

12 *The Occasional Services and Additional Orders* (Minneapolis: Augsburg Publishing House and Board of Publications, Lutheran Church in America, 1962), 100ff.

community to serve in places of great need but few finances. We were connected with each other through daily prayer, both at the Deaconess House chapel, and in our individual prayer times.

The Situation of the North American Lutheran Diaconate Today

There tend to be three varieties of Lutheran deaconesses at this time in North America: those who name themselves as part of a *community* with a central deaconess home which provides for retired and "between calls" deaconesses; those who describe themselves as an association; and a third and newer group instituted by a church body. All groups hold prayer within their community (however that community is described) as an integral part of who they are; they meet as a whole community every couple of years. There have been other groups of deaconesses, but either they have amalgamated or have disappeared due to attrition. The deaconess community of which I am a part is under the authority of the Evangelical Lutheran Church in America, and each deaconess is integrally connected to the synod where we serve and under its authority (in the same way as are pastors). The reciprocal agreements held by the ELCA and the ELCIC make this arrangement possible without undue stress. Our centre is near Philadelphia (soon to move to Chicago).

The second, an association, comes from Valparaiso University. While it used to have an affiliation with the Lutheran Church–Missouri Synod, that church declared that this group was no longer needed, due to their theological stance. They are now an independent Lutheran group of deaconesses serving wherever there is need. Neither community has required vows or community living.

The third group of deaconesses is named the "River Forest" deaconesses, from the city where they have their headquarters. The Lutheran Church–Missouri Synod initiated this group. In Canada there are fourteen deaconesses from the ELCA Deaconess Community, two to three Valparaiso deaconesses, and one River Forest deaconess.

In the ELCA, there are also a growing number of diaconal ministers, trained and set apart for the ministry of *diakonia*. They are both men and women, and have much the same qualifications and requirements as those for the ELCA deaconess community. They are professionally and theologically trained, and are somehow somewhat different than the group of "lay professionals" (Associates In Ministry) in the ELCA.

In the ELCIC, since the disbanding of the Board for Theological Education and Leadership a result of the structural reorganization a couple of years ago, diaconal ministry seems to be sliding into a dark corner. The national church council has instituted a moratorium on diaconal ministry No one may go through the process at this time. Whether we are like one young man who prepared himself according to the guidelines (which he was told was official policy) some three years ago, or whether we have already served in this church for twenty to fifty years as a deaconess, we have been sidetracked, perhaps even hi-jacked. The national Canadian church in convention may have called us into being in 1991, but they obviously don't know what to do with us now. The moratorium simply and graphically illustrates the nature of the relationship and the vacillating understanding within our church in Canada at present.

Wants, Fantasies, and Beliefs — *and Some Nightmares*

> A diaconal minister is called by God and affirmed and recognized by the church, to witness to the Gospel through a public ministry that both exemplifies the servant life, and enables and equips the people of God in their ministries.[13]

---

13 Evangelical Lutheran Church in Canada, *Diaconal Ministry in the ELCIC*, (July 1994), 1.1. This paper has four sections: Diaconal Ministry; Candidacy Process; Preparation and Training; and Support. An additional page shows

> Diaconal ministers are ordained to carry on the apostolic min-
> istry of equipping the whole people of God to exercise their
> Christian calling in daily life and of serving in areas of human
> need in society. Diaconal Ministers do this through special-
> ized knowledge and skills which are placed at the service of
> the church.[14]

The first quotation comes from a paper which "consecrates" diaconal
ministers, the second a guideline which "ordains" diaconal ministers.
By placing these two definitions together we show the very fine line
which has been created by the people of this church. It seems to me
that both definitions portray an ordained diaconate.

I believe I have been ordained a deaconess (into diaconal ministry). I believe God has and continues to call me into this ministry,
part of the one apostolic ministry. I do not believe that as deacon-
esses/diaconal ministers we are "second class," not quite reaching the
standards of presbyter/priest/pastor. I do not believe in that kind of
hierarchy. Years ago I would not have named our consecration/set-
ting apart as ordination — it would not have occurred to me. As it still
is for many people, in my mind ordination was reserved for pastors
only. I now believe that this reservation carries no divine exclusive
command, nor even a Lutheran confessional dictate. I believe that
God worked through the church in the mid-1800s and through the
General Synod in the late 1800s, and through the two recent task
forces, to show what our next step might be.

Whether or not the churches wish to declare that diaconal ministers are "ordained," the church of which I have been a part has effectively treated deaconesses as having been ordained. Because of the
dichotomy between beliefs and actions, the term has never been used.

---

the course of study offered at Waterloo Lutheran Seminary. It has no author
or date, but from its contents I surmise it is post-1993 convention. It is similar to DTEL's "Diaconal Ministry in the ELCIC" as given in Appendix I of
the Minutes for the ELCIC 1993 national convention.
14 "Diaconal Ministry in the ELCIC" — Guidelines for Diaconal Ministry,
Appendix 1, National Convention Minutes, 1993, 284.

How has the church treated the deaconess community as if it were ordained? It has authorized women to be accepted or rejected as deaconesses. It has overseen the deaconess community and the preparation of women for the diaconate. (Our community's process of psychological testing and discernment of call was the pattern for what is now used for pastoral candidates.) The church has provided for the consecration (sometime called "setting apart") of deaconesses. In that liturgical service, hands of pastors, presidents/bishops, and deaconesses were laid on our heads. The prayers were for the indwelling of the Holy Ghost. The expectations of the kind of life, of acceptance of call and the requirement of public commitment are explicitly given in the liturgy recently again entitled "consecration." It has set financial guidelines and we are responsible to the bishop of our synods. We have operated under "call" which is almost identical to that of an ordained pastor. The calling agency (institution, parish, congregation, synod, etc.) must abide by the same rules and regulations as those that are in place for the pastor. Our ministry is a public ministry. We are called to teach and to serve, to equip the people of God for ministry.

In many cases the training required of the deaconess is more than that required for pastoral ministry. We must have an occupation and theological training. When one enters parish work, an education degree is recommended (though not required) with a minimum of two years' theological training in a seminary (Master of Theological Studies or Master of Religious Education). If the occupation is in the Social Services field, then a Master's level education is recommended, or, whatever provides the appropriate professional training for that occupation. Always, theological training is required.

Diaconal ministry has been misunderstood, challenged, wished away, and loved within the Lutheran church in North America. Until the most recent years, only women have performed this "professional" ministry. Until about thirty years ago, pastors (male) were the decision-makers even for our community. Since I became a deaconess the church has seemed to dislike, respect, misunderstand, and cherish the deaconess community. This has often been confusing and difficult to explain to others. We ourselves within the community have had to come to new understandings of who we are and why we serve. We have known whose we are and whom we serve.

Frederick Weiser is well acquainted with our community and with *diakonia* worldwide. Perhaps his words, written in 1984, will further name the reasons for the dichotomy that persists. "No church body in the world has retained this tri-fold ministry of early Christianity in its pristine sense. The titles may remain — as they do in nearly all church bodies — but their content has changed. Lutheranism, for instance, uses all three words, but it has had such a stark emphasis historically on one ministerial office, that of Word and Sacrament, that when it has needed other 'ministers' it has tended to see them as human creations rather than as divine vocations or as a form of public ministry. When the diaconate for men and women was revived in nineteenth century Lutheranism, the ordained clergy were eager to make clear that the deacons and deaconesses belonged to their brotherhood or sisterhood and were not servants of the Church itself."[15]

In Conclusion

At this point in time the diaconate in the American and Canadian Lutheran churches is not an ordained ministry. Nor have recent church conventions indicated a willingness to move towards the ordination of diaconal ministers. Will the churches be able to retract those decisions in the near future? Will we be able to trust each other enough to even consider it? Do we want to be part of other Lutheran churches around the world, or join more closely with other brothers and sisters ecumenically? Perhaps the ecumenical fire will be the spark that will provide a new heat and a new flame. May God make it so.

---

15 Weiser, 35

THE STATE OF THE DIACONATE IN THE ANGLICAN CHURCH OF CANADA

Maylanne Maybee

Introduction

The original essay on this topic was prepared for the Anglican-Lutheran Consultation on the Diaconate in response to an invitation to contribute to a "survey of present theological reflection, concrete structures and possibilities." Specifically, I was asked to describe the *status questionis* relating to the diaconate in my particular church, the Anglican Church of Canada.

I have approached this task somewhat subjectively, though with some reference to the research and reflections of others. Having been active in and vocal about the diaconate since I was ordained sixteen years ago, and having served on most national task forces and contributed to many diocesan and provincial studies relating to the diaconate in the Anglican Church of Canada, it is hard to determine where I left off and they began! Because of its subjectivity, there are many gaps in the picture, particularly relating to the question of direct ordination.

There is little that I will present here that others have not thought of first. When I wrote my M.Div. thesis on the diaconate in 1982, I was greatly influenced by the theology and experience of Wesley Frensdorff (the late Bishop of Nevada) and Deacons Ormonde Plater and Phina Borgeson, who were key actors in the National Center for the Diaconate, now the North American Association for the Diaconate. Edward Schillebeeckx's book, *Ministry: Leadership in the Community of Jesus Christ*, was also formative in my thinking.

Nevertheless, I have tried to do justice to the context, contributions, and current practice relating to the diaconate in the Anglican Church of Canada. I begin with a contextual overview and a review of recent efforts to revive a distinctive diaconate in Canada, drawing on the unique issues with which we are grappling. I then offer a personal reflection and a proposed theological framework for restoring the diaconate. I conclude by briefly describing what is being done in the Diocese of Toronto to reintroduce diaconal ministry.

A word about terminology. I prefer to speak of the "diaconate" or "distinctive diaconate." Adjectives such as "vocational," "permanent," or "perpetual" suggest that the norm is a diaconate to which people are ordained as a condition of their priesthood. This I prefer to call the "transitional diaconate," in spite of protests from priests who treasure the diaconal identity which they associate with their first ordination. My assumption from the outset is that the diaconate can and should be "a full and equal order."

The Cultural Context of the Anglican Church of Canada

It is impossible to separate a theology of the diaconate from the practical experience of ministry in the Anglican Church of Canada. More than the United States, Canada has inherited and clung to the English model of ministry delivery — paid, professional clergy in parish churches. The story of the diaconate in Canada is closely linked to this deeply entrenched pattern of church life.

In the larger, urbanized and more resourced Canadian dioceses there has been a climate of resistance or indifference to the restoration of the diaconate. Where paid clergy abound, parishes have favoured the use of lay volunteers as chalice bearers, pastoral visitors, and church administrators and see the diaconate as an unnecessary clericalization of these roles. Where parishes and diocesan offices have been able to afford it, lay professional workers have been used in what some might consider diaconal functions. Often this group is the most dubious about the introduction of an ordained office which would potentially devalue their role in the church.

In more far-flung and rural dioceses, where seminary-trained priests are in short supply and resources to support them are limited, the general practice has been to use lay readers or catechists (especially in native communities) to lead morning prayer, deliver homilies (their own or one prepared for them), in some cases to administer pre-consecrated bread and wine, and perform other such duties in the absence of professional clergy. In such instances, interest in the diaconate has been as a non-stipendiary supplement to the work of stipendiary priests, "fortified" by the added authority associated with ordination. Understandably, experiments with the diaconate in these circumstances have tended to be confusing and frustrating.

As well, the ordination of women to the priesthood since 1976 has virtually wiped out the tradition of diaconal ministry which for so long was sustained, exemplified, and pioneered by deaconesses. While they served with dedication, usually in places where male clergy would not go, many experienced the bitterness of exploitation and neglect, and are now hardly enthusiastic proponents of the restoration of this order.

In spite of these trends, the question of a distinctive diaconate is one which will not go away. Like the infamous Energizer rabbit, "it keeps going and going and going." Moreover, a radical shift is taking place across Canada in the diocesan, parish, and congregational life of the Anglican church. The reduction of funds and the steady decline in church membership make it increasingly difficult to maintain a model of ministry which relies exclusively on professional, stipendiary clergy. Changes in circumstances are bringing about changes in the theology and practice of ministry and the role of ordained offices within it.

Recent Efforts to Revive a Distinctive Diaconate

In the early 1980s there was a flurry of interest in the diaconate in Canada, attributable perhaps to the influence of what was happening in the Episcopal Church in the United States, to the rethinking surrounding the question of the ordination of women, and to the work of preparing *The Book of Alternative Services*. Several studies and task forces were commissioned to study the place of the diaconate in the church's ministry and to make recommendations.

In 1982 the diocese of Cariboo sponsored a consultation on the diaconate for the ecclesiastical province of British Columbia and Yukon. Dan Meakes, a deacon in Cariboo at the time, produced an excellent and still topical paper which he called *The Diaconate: Servanthood Not Slavery*.[1] Bruce Pellegrin, a priest in the diocese of Ottawa, produced a thoughtful study on *The Diaconate as Vocation and Ministry*, again in 1982.[2] The diocese of Niagara struck a task force, which ultimately recommended no action, again in 1982. That same year, the ecclesiastical province of Ontario sponsored a widely attended consultation for bishops and senior clergy in Ontario. However, no clear consensus or direction arose out of these events.

Many, if not most, of these efforts have since faded into the background, though some continuity was sustained by the General Synod and its Committee on Ministry. Recently, there has been a noticeable revival of activity in pockets across Canada.

At General Synod in 1986, a resolution authorized a task force to prepare guidelines for the restoration of a distinctive diaconate. The task force guidelines were adopted handily at the subsequent General Synod of 1989.[3]

Since the mid-1970s the ecclesiastical province of Ontario has had an effective moratorium against ordination to the so-called "permanent diaconate." In 1991 the moratorium was officially lifted when the provincial synod of Ontario accepted a set of guidelines, based on the 1989 General Synod report. Since then, the diocese of Toronto,

---

1 Dan E. Meakes, *The Diaconate: Servanthood Not Slavery: A Position Paper on the Restoration of the Holy Order of Deacons in the Diocese of Cariboo* (April 1982).

2 Bruce Pellegrin, *The Diaconate as Vocation and Ministry: A Paper prepared at the Request of the Bishop of Ottawa for the House of Bishops Meeting in Aylmer, Québec, October, 1982.*

3 Committee on Ministry, *A Plan to Restore the Diaconate in the Anglican Church of Canada* (Toronto, ON: Anglican Church of Canada, 1989).

under the initial leadership of Bishop Joachim Fricker, struck its own task force which was charged to develop a practical plan to introduce a distinctive diaconate. In April 1994, I was contracted by the diocese to staff this initiative.

Recent activities I am aware of are a clergy event on the diaconate in the diocese of Rupert's Land in December 1994 and a consultation on the diaconate sponsored by the diocese of Montréal for the ecclesiastical province of Canada in the fall of 1994. Steps are also being explored in Rupert's Land. By contrast, a resolution to reinstitute the diaconate in the diocese of Niagara (based in Hamilton, Ontario) was defeated at their synod in October 1994.

In 1996 the bishops of the ecclesiastical province of Canada issued a statement calling for the restoration of the diaconate in the province.[4] There is movement in this direction in every diocese of the province. Montréal, Eastern Newfoundland and Labrador, and Nova Scotia have established commissions on the diaconate, ordained a number of deacons, and taken steps toward the establishment of a community of deacons within their dioceses and province.

The early consultations on the diaconate in the ecclesiastical province of British Columbia and Yukon have begun to bear fruit.[5] In 1993 the diocesan synod of New Westminster gave approval to guidelines for the restoration of the diaconate. Since the approval of these guidelines the diaconal community has grown to thirteen. Similar developments have taken place in the diocese of British Columbia with a diaconal community that numbers six at this time.

These disparate measures reflect the polity of the Anglican church in Canada. In spite of leadership given by General Synod, it has no binding jurisdiction over individual dioceses, who can act or not act as they choose. And unless there is commitment or at least permissive

---

4 The information in this paragraph was supplied by the Rt. Rev. Fred Hiltz, Suffragan Bishop of Nova Scotia.

5 The information in this paragraph was supplied by the Rev. Dr. Richard G. Leggett, Coordinator of Diaconal Formation in the Diocese of New Westminster.

neutrality on the part of a diocesan bishop, there is little possibility of establishing a common understanding and practice of selecting, ordaining, and using deacons.

Theological and Practical Issues

The criteria applied by Dan Meakes for developing a position concerning the diaconate in his above mentioned paper on the diaconate are worth repeating here. What is required is a framework for the diaconate which is consistent with our context for ministry, consistent with tradition, and effective in its implications.

According to Meakes, the question is, can we establish a servanthood within an institution, a community, the church, which has historically been oriented to self preservation? The re-establishment of the diaconate challenges the very integrity of the Christian community and its willingness to live out Christ's example of ministry among the poor. He points to the largely middle class membership of the church, and the church's preference to associate mission with evangelism rather than caring for the poor.

> There are many practical choices to be made with respect to the diaconate which have vast theological implications. Deacons ordained for the sake of a multitude of convenient reasons will result in slavery. Deacons in the context of renewal of mission and the total ministry of the laos have the potential of establishing a new relationship between Church and World, or Christian Community and dominant Society.... We will hope that our practical decisions are faithful to the ministry of servanthood expressed by Christ.[6]

---

6 Meakes, 2.

Meakes speaks with the voice of one in a frontier diocese having a variety of communities and needs, and a close association with the Episcopal Church in the United States. Bruce Pellegrin, who wrote a paper the same year for the bishop of Ottawa, speaks in the context of an urban diocese in Ontario, the largest, most populated, and until recently most resourced province in Canada. He argues with the voice of one formed by a more settled church, that "the needs of society demonstrate a subtle but real calling of the church to make present the servanthood-caring of the Christian community and that this can be best effected by persons who know themselves to be specially called and commissioned to that function."[7]

My own position combines the passion of Meakes with the caution of Pellegrin. The church must decide what it wants to do and develop the leadership to support it. At present, the situation does not encourage Anglicans to engage in diaconal ministry or to consider the diaconate as a vocation. The diocesan, congregational, and parish structures of the church are designed to support the gathered, worshipping life of the Christian community. Capital resources are used to maintain or construct buildings for worship, Christian education, and congregational fellowship. Resources for education are used to support theological colleges preparing students for parish priesthood. Training and continuing education opportunities emphasize skills in liturgy, preaching, Christian education, individual pastoral care, and counselling.

As Pellegrin points out, "The present structures appear to force a candidate for ordination into accepting priesthood or nothing. They are surrounded by models of ministry geared toward the presbyterate, they are faced by institutions who see the presbyterate as the ultimate goal, they deal with Diocesan Structures and Canon law that presuppose presbyteral ordination and stipend."[8]

---

7 Pellegrin, 2.
8 Ibid., 9.

It would not be accurate to imply there is nothing in place to support leadership in ministries of justice and social care. The church has done remarkable work among natives, refugees, people with AIDS. The Canadian Urban Training Project (CUT) trained scores of clergy and laity alike in skills of analysis, social change, and building partnerships with people of low income. The Centre for Christian Studies has trained women and men from the Anglican and United churches in diaconal and social justice ministries, though few (if any) Anglicans have gone on to be deacons.

But the systemic bias toward the presbyterate is reinforced by the economic structure of the church. Whereas parish ministries and many chaplaincies can be self-supporting, diaconal ministry not only does not contribute to the material life of the church, it actually costs it money. Opportunities to do professional ministry in areas of justice, advocacy, and peace-making among poor and marginal people are generally limited to positions in para-ecclesiastical organizations which pay less, are less secure, and usually require higher levels of accountability and justification.

The larger issue is that this aspect of the Church's ministry is not closely related to congregational life, and is not adequately upheld as the work of the entire Church and calling of all Christians. Indeed, because professional priesthood is the dominant model for ministry, "lay ministry" tends to be regarded as an extension of priestly functions by volunteers. The term is widely used either to describe what lay people are allowed to do in the liturgy or in reference to what non-ordained professionals are paid to do in the institutional church.

A Personal Reflection

My vision of the diaconate is based on an understanding that Christians are baptized into ministry which is the work of the *laos* in the Church and in the world. This includes not only the gathered, worshipping life of the Church, but also the dispersed, "sent forth" mission of the Church. *Diakonia* is that expression of Christian ministry which has to do with our baptismal vows to proclaim the good news of God in Christ, to seek and serve Christ in all persons, to strive for peace and justice among all people, to respect the dignity of every human being. Servanthood in particular is shown forth in caring for the *anawim* or "little ones" of society without expectation of return.

So here is my theology of the diaconate. Christian communities have within them the gifts and means to order their sacramental life. Within that sacramental life, bishops give symbolic focus and practical leadership to the apostolic Church in areas relating to oversight, unity, tradition, catholicism, and ecumenism. Presbyters give symbolic focus and practical leadership to the local, gathered Church in its life of worship, fellowship, and reconciliation.

In the same way, deacons are needed to give symbolic focus and practical leadership to the "sent forth" Church in its mission of service, proclamation, peace, and justice-making. What we are talking about is not another layer of clericalism, but another kind of leadership, one that is directed outward, that supports people in defining and undertaking intentional ministry in their daily lives, and that continually calls the Church to look beyond itself, to the world which Jesus loved and loves.

Skeptics about the diaconate often ask, "Why should we ordain deacons to do what lay people can do already?" This gets at the heart of the confusion about ordination. The influence of a professional class of priestly clergy has given lay people the powerful message that there are certain things they cannot or are not allowed to do. Priesthood is commonly understood as something in the possession of certain individuals through ordination, rather than something which belongs to the whole people of God through baptism. The assumption is that priests are ordained to consecrate bread and wine, to baptize, marry and bury, and to dispense blessings and absolutions. We say that priests "celebrate the eucharist," that they "marry" couples, that they "absolve" sinners. In this view, ordination is seen to confer special powers and privileges that other baptized Christians do not possess.

It is possible, and I believe desirable, to understand ordination differently. If priesthood is viewed as a characteristic of the people of

God, then it is the gathered people of God who celebrate the eucharist, it is the couple who do the marrying, it is God-in-community who absolves and reconciles the broken and alienated. The church does not ordain people to do these things on behalf of or instead of other baptized Christians, but to preside over and give leadership to their corporate authority which is sealed by baptism. This is why there is a recovery of the use of the word "presbyter" which has a less sacerdotal connotation than "priest."

Ordination is the church's way of selecting and designating a person to whom the community has entrusted a practical and symbolic leadership role. Presbyters (literally, "elders," people with seniority) are entrusted to gather, preside, and give focus to the common Christian life of a worshipping community. They should be able to help a community develop a sense of corporate ("pastoral") identity, to demonstrate mutual care, to strengthen unity, and overcome divisions. They express this liturgically by calling the community to worship, pronouncing (not dispensing!) absolution and blessing, and presiding at important events, such as weddings, baptisms, and funerals, in the lives of individuals and the community.

In the same way, ordination to the diaconate is the church's way of selecting and designating people who are called by their community to give leadership in mission and service. The ordination service for deacons in *The Book of Alternative Services* defines the diaconate in three ways which make it distinct from the priesthood:

1. It is a special ministry of servanthood, directly under the authority of the bishop. Deacons are accountable to their bishop as servants who support the bishop's oversight of the church in mission. Presbyters work together with their bishop and fellow presbyters and share in the councils of the church.

2. It is a ministry of service to all people, particularly the poor, the weak, the sick and the lonely. Deacons have a particular responsibility for those who are vulnerable. Presbyters are entrusted to care alike for young and old, strong and weak, rich and poor.

3. It is a ministry of interpretation to the church of the needs, concerns, and hopes of the world. Presbyters have a ministry to be "a pastor, priest, and teacher."

Thus, the qualities, work, and spiritual gifts of a person who is recognized to be the community's deacon should be visibly connected with the liturgical and symbolic role entrusted to them. Deacons are chosen for their ability to support people to tell their story as baptized Christians, to invite prayers for and practical responses to those who are poor, lonely, sick or dying, to identify personal gifts and community resources, and direct them toward opportunities for service.

These abilities have a logical connection with the eucharistic acts of proclaiming the gospel, leading the intercessions, receiving the offering, doing table service, dismissing the people. Deacons are also appropriate eucharistic ministers to those who are sick, dying, or shut in.

And all this with an understanding that true lay ministry is the ministry of the *laos*, the whole people of God, and true liturgy is the life work of the Church and its members.

Practical Applications

The challenge, of course, is to give concrete realization to this vision. It means helping people to unpack and unlearn deeply held assumptions. It means the retirement of a generation or two of clergy whose self-understanding is more sacerdotal than presbyteral. It means helping people to unlearn that "ministry" is what clergy do in the church, and to convince them that it is what they do in their lives. And it means leading the church to look beyond its nose to the society of change, need, suffering, and hope around it.

This kind of re-ordering of Christian community is required before there will be room for deacons and support for the full diaconal ministry of the Church. One model is that of "mutual" or "total" ministry which is being applied and practised in US dioceses such as

Nevada, Alaska, and Northern Michigan, and is being somewhat more tentatively introduced into Canadian dioceses such as Qu'Appelle or Algoma.

My own experience is with the diocese of Toronto which, unlike those dioceses practising "total ministry," does not (yet) have a large number of underfunded congregations and does not suffer from a shortage of professional, seminary-trained clergy. It is, however, in the throes of financial cutbacks which are likely to change these conditions over the next ten years.

When the ecclesiastical province of Ontario adopted guidelines for a distinctive diaconate and lifted the moratorium against ordaining people to be deacons who did not intend to become presbyters, the diocese of Toronto struck a task force which met for two years to study different models and to establish diocesan guidelines and procedures before hiring a coordinator (myself) to put them into practice. Several features of these guidelines and procedures are worth noting:

1. The revival process is one of both an office and a ministry. Individuals will not be ordained deacons except in a context where the community to which they relate are prepared to share in diaconal ministry.

2. For this reason, individuals cannot "self-select" to become deacons. Application must be made by the parish, with the full endorsement of the incumbent and advisory board. An important part of the approach we are using is to provide congregations with the educational and discernment tools they need to nominate and work with a candidate and ordinand to the diaconate.

3. Deacons will be expected to serve, at least initially, in the communities which nominate them. They are officers of the wider church, but not in isolation from a worshipping community which authorizes them to serve. In cases where a deacon moves, it will be the decision of the bishop and the receiving community whether that person will be licensed to an active diaconate.

4. "Formation" and "training" are understood to be separate but inter-related components in the preparation and support of individuals for diaconal ministry. All candidates will undergo a similar formation process, which will help them to understand their identity as deacons, their liturgical role, and their relationships in and outside the church (to bishops, presbyters, other deacons, other baptized Christians, as well as with families, work colleagues, the unbaptized). It is assumed that deacons will already have some kind of professional identity and training (as teachers, nurses, firefighters, chaplains, or whatever). Additional training requirements will vary according to the individual and their context for ministry. In some cases, they will need to develop skills which will help them in their interpretive role, such as small group leadership, social analysis, community organizing, conflict resolution, adult education, and public speaking. These are to be determined in consultation with an assigned mentor and the worshipping community. Deacons are not expected to have a different level of expertise in disciplines such as scripture, doctrine, church history, or spirituality than other baptized Christians. If they want to increase their fluency in any of these areas, they are encouraged to do so with others in their community, for their personal growth and faith development.

5. Deacons will not normally be employees of the church, though there are some instances where this will be desirable. They will be discouraged from identifying themselves as "clergy," though this category is still strong in the mind of Canadian Anglicans. This means that they will refrain from using clerical titles and dress, and will not qualify for benefits (housing allowance, pension, tax breaks, etc.) extended to clergy except if they are employees of the church. My preference is that deacons will be given voice and not vote at synod, preferably in the context of "interpreting the needs, hopes and concerns of the world" at a given point in the synod agenda. The standard for time given directly to the church

will be eight hours a week. Compensation or honoraria for travel, continuing education and related costs is to be negotiated between the parish, the diocese, and the individual.

6. Toronto has chosen to introduce models of how the diaconate might work in particular settings, and to show by example the difference they can make to the life and mission of the church. Because we are developing a process rather than a program, these features are being piloted on a small scale in three parishes across the diocese. After some evaluation, opportunities to explore the diaconate will be made available gradually and organically to other parishes expressing need or interest. Members of diocesan synod have been fully informed of the work of the task force, but the bishops were the ones to give approval to proceed. Clergy were invited to a learning and reflection day on the diaconate which allowed them to raise questions, express concerns, and contribute suggestions.

To conclude, let me associate myself with remarks made by Peter Flynn in his article "Diaconate from a Priest's Point of View" that appeared in *Rupert's Land News*.

Of course, the restoration of the diaconate raises issues demanding discussion and resolution, such as vocation, discernment, training, accountability, support and supervision, dress, salary, and tasks, to name a few. However, since I am traditionalist enough to reject the suggestion made by some that the Anglican Church should abolish the order, I would rather that we engage in what I think already is an important, not to say exciting venture of restoring the diaconate to the church. I think action on reviving the diaconate as a sign to the church of its vocation to servanthood in Christ has a role in the increasing discussions about ministry in the church today.

APPENDIX 1:

Lambeth Conference Resolutions on Anglican-Lutheran Relations

Lambeth Conference 1888

Resolution 14: That, in the opinion of this Conference, earnest efforts should be made to establish more friendly relations between the Scandinavian and Anglican Churches; and that approaches on the part of the Swedish Church, with a view to the mutual explanation of differences, be most gladly welcomed, in order to the ultimate establishment, if possible, of intercommunion on sound principles of ecclesiastical polity.

Lambeth Conference 1897

Resolution 39: That this Conference, being desirous of furthering the action taken by the Lambeth Conference of 1888 with regard to the validity of the orders of the Swedish Church, requests the Archbishop of Canterbury to appoint a committee to inquire into the question, and to report to the next Lambeth Conference; and that it is desirable that the committee, if appointed, should confer with the authorities or representatives of the Church of Sweden upon the subject of the proposed investigation.

Lambeth Conference 1908

Resolution 74: This Conference heartily thanks the Archbishop of Upsala for his letter of friendly greeting, and for sending his honoured colleague, the Bishop of Kalmar, to confer with its members on the question of the establishment of an alliance of some sort between the Swedish and Anglican Churches. The Conference respectfully desires the Archbishop of Canterbury to appoint a commission to correspond further with the Swedish Church through the Archbishop of Upsala on the possibility and conditions of such an alliance.

Lambeth Conference 1920

Resolution 24: The Conference welcomes the Report of the Commission appointed after the last Conference entitled "The Church of England and the Church of Sweden," and, accepting the conclusions there maintained on the succession of bishops of the Church of Sweden and the conception of the priesthood set forth in its standards, recommends that members of that Church, qualified to receive the sacrament in their own Church, should be admitted to Holy Communion in ours. It also recommends that on suitable occasions permission should be given to Swedish ecclesiastics to give addresses in our churches. If the authorities of any province of the Anglican Communion find local irregularities in the order or practice of the Church of Sweden outside that country, they may legitimately, within their own region, postpone any such action as is recommended in this Resolution until they are satisfied that these irregularities have been removed.

Resolution 25: We recommend further that in the event of an invitation being extended to an Anglican bishop or bishops to take part in the consecration of a Swedish bishop, the invitation should, if possible, be accepted, subject to the approval of the metropolitan. We also recommend that, in the first instance, as an evident token of the restoration of closer relations between the two Churches, if possible more than one of our bishops should take part in the consecration.

Lambeth Conference 1930

Resolution 37: The Conference thanks the Church of Sweden for the visit of the Bishop of Lund and expresses its hope that the existing fraternal relations with that Church will be maintained, and that relations may also be strengthened with the other Scandinavian Churches with a view to promoting greater unity in the future.

Resolution 38: The Conference requests the Archbishop of Canterbury, as soon as seems advisable, to appoint a committee to investigate the position of the Church of Finland and its relations to the Church of England.

Lambeth Conference 1948

Resolution 69: The Conference welcomes the steady growth in friendship between the Scandinavian Churches and the Anglican Communion. It calls attention to the Resolutions adopted by the Conference of 1920 concerning relations with the Church of Sweden and recommends that they be formally brought to the notice of such Churches and provinces of the Anglican Communion as have not yet considered them.

Resolution 70: The Conference receives with approval the Report of the committee appointed by the Archbishop of Canterbury to confer with representatives of the Church of Finland, published in 1934, notes the conclusion reached in that Report and recommends that the Report, together with the recommendations, be brought to the attention of such Churches and provinces of the Anglican Communion as have not yet considered them.

Resolution 71: The Conference receives the Report of conferences between representatives appointed by the Archbishop of Canterbury on behalf of the Church of England and representatives of the Evangelical Lutheran Churches of Latvia and Estonia in 1936 and 1938, published in 1938. It records its sympathy and offers its prayers for these Churches, many of whose clergy and laity are now scattered abroad, having no home or possessions of their own, and having suffered grievous hardship. It recommends that Anglicans should give all material and spiritual help possible to these unhappy exiles, and looks forward to the day when it will be possible, after full agreement in faith and order, to advance further the relations between the Anglican Communion and these Churches in conditions of mutual confidence and understanding.

Resolution 72: The Conference requests the Archbishop of Canterbury to appoint a committee to confer with a similar committee or committees representing the Churches of Norway, Denmark, and Iceland, for the purpose of considering the relations of these Churches with the Anglican Communion.

Lambeth Conference 1958

Resolution 48: The Conference welcomes the action taken by several Churches and provinces in accordance with Resolutions 69, 70 and 71 of the Lambeth Conference of 1948.

Lambeth Conference 1968

Resolution 59: The Conference recommends the initiation of Anglican-Lutheran conversations on a world-wide basis as soon as possible.

Lambeth Conference 1978

Resolution 31: The Conference encourages Anglican Churches together with Lutheran Churches in their area: 1. to study the report entitled "Anglican-Lutheran International Conversations" (the Pullach Report, 1972), Resolution 22 of the second meeting (Dublin, 1973) and Resolution 5 of the third meeting (Trinidad, 1976) of the Anglican Consultative Council; 2. to give special attention to our ecclesial recognition of the Lutheran Church on the basis of these reports and resolutions; and 3. to seek ways of extending hospitality and of engaging in joint mission.

Lambeth Conference 1988

Resolution 14: This Conference

1. Receives with gratitude the "Cold Ash Report" (1983) of the Anglican-Lutheran Joint Working Group and approves its recommendations (see "Emmaus Report," pp. 82–84).

2. Welcomes the "Niagara Report" of the Anglican-Lutheran Consultation on "Episcope" (1987), recognizes in it a substantial convergence of views, and commends it to the member Churches of the Anglican Communion for study and synodical reception.

3. Recommends that the permanent body already established by the Anglican Consultative Council and the Lutheran World Federation to co-ordinate and assess developing Anglican-Lutheran relationships (the Anglican/Lutheran International Continuation Committee) be renamed as the Anglican-Lutheran International Commission, and asked to undertake the following tasks in addition to its existing terms of reference:

> (a) to integrate in a broader document the theological work already accomplished in international, regional and local dialogues;
> (b) to explore more thoroughly the theological and canonical requirements that are necessary in both Churches to acknowledge and recognise the full authenticity of existing ministries (see "Niagara Report", para. 94);
> (c) to advise with sensitivity on the actual pastoral practices of our Churches in regard to the celebration of God's word and sacraments, especially the Holy Eucharist;
> (d) to produce a report which will indicate the degree of convergence of views on the ordained ministry of bishops, presbyters and deacons.

4. Recognises, on the basis of the high degree of consensus reached in international, regional and national dialogues between Anglicans and Lutherans and in the light of the communion centred around word and sacrament that has been experienced in each other's traditions, the presence of the Church of Jesus Christ in the Lutheran Communion as our own.

5. Urges that this recognition and the most recent convergence on apostolic ministry achieved in the "Niagara Report" of the Anglican-Lutheran Consultation on "Episcope" (1987) prompt us to move towards the fullest possible ecclesial recognition and the goal of full communion.

6. Recommends to member Churches, subject to the concurence of the Lutheran World Federation, that:

(a) Anglican and Lutheran Churches should officially establish and encourage the practice of mutual eucharistic hospitality — if this is not already authorised — where pastoral need exists and when ecumenical occasions make this appropriate;

(b) The provinces of our Communion should make provision for appropriate forms of 'interim eucharistic sharing' along the following lines:

(i) They should by synodical action recognize now the member Churches of the Lutheran World Federation as Churches in which the Gospel is preached and taught;

(ii) They should encourage the development of common Christian life throughout their respective Churches by such means as the following proposals of the "Niagara Report":

(a) eucharistic sharing and joint common celebration of the Eucharist;

(b) meetings of Church leaders for regular prayer, reflection and consultation, thus beginning joint episcope;

(c) mutual invitation of Church leaders, clergy and laity, to synods, with a right to speak;

(d) common agencies wherever possible;

(e) exploring the possibility of adjusting boundaries to assist local and regional co-operation;

(f) covenants among Church leaders to collaborate in episcope;

(g) joint pastoral appointments for special projects;

(h) joint theological education and training courses;

(i) sharing of information and documents;

(j) joint mission programmes;

(k) agreed syllabuses for Christian education in schools, joint materials for catechesis and adult study;

(l) co-operation over liturgical forms, cycle of intercession, lectionaries and homiletic materials;

(m) welcoming isolated clergy or diaspora congregations into the life of a larger group (see ALERC "Helsinki Report," 5);
(n) interchange of ministers to the extent permitted by canon law;
(o) twinning (partnership) between congregations and communities;
(p) joint programmes of diaconal ministry and reflection on issues of social responsibility;
(q) joint retreats and devotional materials.

(iii) They should affirm by synodical action now on the basis of the consensus documents of Anglican-Lutheran International Conversations that the basic teaching of each respective Church is consonant with Scripture and that Lutheran teaching is sufficiently compatible with the teachings of the Churches of the Anglican Communion so that a relationship of interim sharing of the Eucharist may be established between these Churches under the guidelines appended.

Notes: Guidelines for the Interim Sharing of the Eucharist

(a) The Churches of the Anglican Communion extend a special welcome to members of the Lutheran Churches to receive Holy Communion on the understanding that the Lutheran Churches will do likewise. This welcome constitutes a recognition of eucharistic teaching sufficient for interim sharing of the Eucharist.

(b) Bishops of dioceses of the Anglican Communion and bishops/presidents of Lutheran districts and synods may by mutual agreement extend their regulations of church discipline to permit common, joint celebration of the Eucharist within their jurisdictions according to guidelines established by respective synods. In this case: When a joint Eucharist is held in an Anglican church an Anglican bishop or priest should preside, using an Anglican liturgy, with the Lutheran preaching; when a joint Eucharist is held in a Lutheran church a Lutheran should preside using a Lutheran liturgy, with the Anglican preaching. This is not concelebration, nor does it imply rejection or final recognition of either Church's eucharist or ministry. The liturgical arrangements, including the position of the ministers in relation to the alter, should take into account local circumstances and sensitivities. (See further paras. 72–78 and para. 82b of the Report on "Ecumenical Relations.")

Lambeth Conference 1998

Resolution IV.1: This Conference

a. reaffirms the Anglican commitment to the full, visible unity of the Church as the goal of the Ecumenical Movement;

b. encourages the further explication of the characteristics which belong to the full, visible unity of the Church (described variously as the goal, the marks, or the portrait of visible unity); and

c. recognises that the process of moving towards full, visible unity may entail temporary anomalies, and believes that some anomalies may be bearable when there is an agreed goal of visible unity, but that there should always be an impetus towards their resolution and, thus, towards the removal of the principal anomaly of disunity.

Resolution IV.2: This Conference

a. reaffirms the Chicago-Lambeth Quadrilateral (1888) as a basis on which Anglicans seek the full, visible unity of the Church, and also recognises it as a statement of Anglican unity and identity;

b. acknowledges that ecumenical dialogues and experience have led to a developing understanding of each of the elements of the Quadrilateral, including the significance of apostolicity, pastoral oversight (episcope), the office of bishop and the historic espiscopate; and

c. commends continuing reflection upon the Quadrilateral's contribution to the search for the full, visible unity of the Church, and in particular the role within visible unity of a common ministry of oversight exercised in personal, collegial and communal ways at every level.

Resolution IV.6: This Conference

a. recommends that the proposed Inter-Anglican Standing Commission on Ecumenical Relations reflect upon the implications of being in communion with the See of Canterbury with particular reference to the United Churches and Churches in Communion;

b. welcomes the fact that the International Bishops' Conference of the Union of Utrecht and the ACC have agreed to the establishment of an Anglican-Old Catholic International Co-ordinating Council;

c. recommends that consideration be given to ways of deepening our communion with the Old Catholic Churches beyond the Bonn Agreement, including means of taking counsel and making decisions together; the anomaly of overlapping jurisdictions; the implications of wider ecumenical relationships, particularly with the Roman Catholic, Orthodox and Lutheran Churches; and the importance of work together on issues of mission and common witness;

d. welcomes the adoption by both churches of the Concordat between the Episcopal Church in the Philippines and the Philippine Independent Church (1997), which establishes a relationship of full communion;

e. welcomes the relationship of communion established in Northern Europe between six Lutheran churches (Estonia, Finland, Iceland, Lithuania, Norway and Sweden) and four Anglican churches (England, Ireland, Scotland and Wales) by the signing of the Porvoo Declaration in 1996, and recognises the enrichment brought through the presence of Finnish, Norwegian and Swedish bishops at this Conference as bishops in communion; and

f. welcomes the decision by the Porvoo Church Leaders Meeting in 1998 that the Lusitanian Catholic Apostolic Evangelical Church of Portugal and the Spanish Episcopal Reformed Church should be regarded as being covered by the Preamble to Porvoo Delaration subject to their Synods' approval of the Declaration.

Resolutuion IV.16: This Conference

a. welcomes the remarkable progress in Anglican-Lutheran relationships during the last decade in many parts of the world;

b. commends for study the report of the Anglican-Lutheran International Commission, The Diaconate as Ecumenical Opportunity (1996);

c. noting the approval by the Episcopal Church in the United States of America of the Concordat of Agreement with the Evangelical Lutheran Church in America and the narrow vote against the Concordat by the ELCA, hopes that the draft revision of the Concordat, currently being undertaken by the ELCA in consultation with representatives from ECUSA, will provide a firm basis for the two churches to move to full communion;

d. commends the progress toward full communion between the Anglican Church of Canada and the Evangelical Lutheran Church in Canada as set forth in the Waterloo Declaration (1997) for consideration by both churches in 2001;

e. encourages the continuation of close relations with the Lutheran Churches of Denmark and Latvia, which participated fully in the Porvoo Conversations but have not so far become signatories;

f. welcomes the development of dialogue in Australia, and of dialogue and collaboration in the search for justice and human rights and the joint pastoral care of scattered Christian communities in Africa;

g. affirms the growing fellowship between churches of the Anglican and Lutheran Communions in other regions of the world, and encourages further steps toward agreement in faith, eucharistic sharing and common mission on the way to the goal of full, visible unity;

h. rejoices not only in the Porvoo Common Statement between the Anglican Churches of Britain and Ireland and the Lutheran Churches of the Nordic and Baltic region, but also in the Meissen Common

Statement with the Evangelical Church in Germany, which includes Lutheran, Reformed and United Churches, and looks forward to the proposed agreement between the Anglican churches of Britain and Ireland and the French Lutheran and Reformed churches; and

i. recommends consultation with the Lutheran World Federation about the continuation of the work of the Anglican Lutheran International Commission.

APPENDIX 2
Anglican Consultative Council Resolutions on Anglican-Lutheran Relations

Anglican Consultative Council (July 1973)

Resolution 2: This Council
(i) receives with satisfaction the Report of the Anglican-Lutheran International Conversations (1970/72) and commends it to the member Churches for consideration;

(ii) approves of the setting up of the Anglican-Lutheran Joint Working Group to receive and examine the comments from the Churches; and to take account of other inter-Church conversations in which Anglicans and Lutherans are involved;

(iii) recommends that it will be essential to allow proper time for the Churches to report their response to the Joint Working Group.[1]

Anglican Consultative Council (March/April 1976)

Resolution 5: The Council welcomes the careful and detailed report of the Joint Working Group. It notes that the responses of Lutheran and Anglican churches to the "Anglican-Lutheran International Conversations" (Pullach Report) make it clear that while there is wide

---

1 Anglican Consultative Council, *Partners in Mission: Report of the Second Meeting, Dublin, Ireland, 17–22 July 1973* (London, UK: SPCK for the Anglican Consultative Council, 1973).

agreement between the two traditions, there are still areas that call for much fuller discussion, especially the concepts of justification, eucharistic presence, apostolicity and episcopacy. In connection with the last point, we hope that attention will be given to the place of bishops in the Church, rather than to the abstract idea of episcope. It is noted that the Joint Working Group does not recommend a further round of international discussions at present, but that local and regional conversations should go on. It is noted also that both Churches are in conversation with the Roman Catholic Church, and the Council hopes that these conversations will lead to a convergence between Anglicans and Lutherans with each other, as well as with Rome.[2]

Anglican Consultative Council (September 1981)

Resolution 2: The Council invites the Lutheran World Federation to consider the reconvening of a Joint Anglican-Lutheran Working Group to assess the regional dialogues and to make appropriate recommendations about the future relationship between the two churches to the Lutheran World Federation and ACC-6.[3]

Anglican Consultative Council (July 1984)

Resolution 25: This Council commends the Report of the Anglican/Lutheran Working Group Anglican-Lutheran Relations, to the member Churches and on its basis:

    (a) recommends that Anglican Churches should officially encourage the practice of eucharistic hospitality to Lutherans — if this is not already authorized — where pastoral need exists and when ecumenical situations make this appropriate;

---

2 Anglican Consultative Council, *Report of the Third Meeting: Trinidad,* 23 March–2 April 1976 (London, UK: Anglican Consultative Council, 1976).
3. Anglican Consultative Council, *Report of the Fifth Meeting: Newcastle upon Tyne, England,* 8–18 September 1981 (London, UK: Angican Consultative Council, 1981).

(b) recommends that as a further step towards full communion, where there is already some degree of mutual ecclesial recognition based on agreement in faith and a commitment to unity, the churches should conside making provision for appropriate forms of "interim eucharistic sharing" along the lines of that authorized in the USA and recommended in Europe;

(c) endorses the proposals for closer collaboration between the ACC and The Lutheran World Federation and their staff set out in Anglican-Lutheran Relations Recommendations IIa-f as financial circumstances may permit.[4]

Resolution 34: In view of the fact that a reduction in the ecumenical budget of 15,000 [pounds sterling] would entail the serious curtailment of the work of the Anglican Centre in Rome or the cancellation of the proposed first meeting of a newly constituted Anglican/Orthodox Commission or the cancellation of the scheduled meeting of ARCIC II together with continuation of working groups with the Lutherans and the Reformed; and in view of the fact that the ecumenical dialogues should not be curtailed by unilateral Anglican action, we recommend that the Standing Committee be authorized to restore as much as is necessary of the 15,000 [pounds sterling] to maintain the ecumenical commitment of the Council if the special appeal meet with success.[5]

Anglican Consultative Council (July/August 1990)

Resolution 15: This Council resolves that the name of the Anglican-Lutheran international dialogue be changed from "The Anglican-Lutheran International Continuation Committee (ALICC)" to "The Anglican-Luteran International Commission," in response to Resolution 4.3 of the Lambeth Conference 1988 ("The truth shall make you

---

4 Anglican Consultative Council, *Proceeding of ACC–6, Badagry, Nigeria, 1984* (London, UK: Anglican Consultative Council, 1984).
5 Ibid.

free," p. 204) and the action of the Executive Committee of the Lutheran World Federation.[6]

Joint Meeting of the Primates of the Anglican Communion and the Anglican Consultative Council (January 1993)

Resolution 8: Resolved, that this Joint Meeting of the Primates of the Anglican Communion and the Anglican Consultative Council warmly welcomes the proposed Anglican/Lutheran Agreements in both the USA and Europe and recommends that the ACC: Send to the Member Churches of the Anglican Communion and the Churches in Full Communion the text of the Episcopal-Lutheran dialogue in the USA, "Towards Full Communion and Concordat of Agreement, 1991" and "The Porvoo Common Statement," the text of the conversations between the Church of England, the Church in Wales, the Episcopal Church of Scotland, the Church of Ireland and the Nordic and Baltic Lutheran Churches, together with the Apostolicity and Succession document of the Church of England by the end of 1993 for study, comment and report back to the Anglican Consultative Council and to the Provinces concerned.[7]

---

6 Anglican Consultative Council, *Mission in a Broken World: Report of ACC–8 Wales, 1990* (London, UK: Church House Publishing for the Anglican Consultative Council, 1990).

7 Anglican Consultative Council, *A Transforming Vision: The Official Report of the Joint Meeting of the Primates of the Anglican Communion and the Anglican Consultative Council* (London, UK: Church House Publishing for the Anglican Communion, 1993).

APPENDIX 3
Lutheran World Federation Resolutions on Anglican–Lutheran Relations

Ninth Assembly, Hong Kong (8–16 July 1997)

Having noted the decisive official steps and various stages of reception that had already been taken between LWF member churches and churches of the Anglican Communion, and been informed of other discussions which were nearing completion, the Council voted:

— to reaffirm and renew commitment to the goal of full communion with churches of the Anglican Communion and urged LWF member churches to take appropriate steps toward the realisations of that goal; and

— to affirm the continuation of the Anglican-Lutheran International Commission and urged it to stimulate and assist the churches to take action which would lead, in appropriate ways, to the furtherance of full communion.

Furthermore, the Council noted with thanksgiving the Anglican-Lutheran agreements already in place and encouraged ever deepening relationships.